Shifting Obsessions

Shifting Obsessions

Three Essays on the Politics of Anticorruption

by
IVAN KRASTEV

With a Foreword by
ARYEH NEIER

CEU PRESS

Central European University Press
Budapest   New York

©2004 by Ivan Krastev

Published in 2004 by

Central European University Press
An imprint of the
Central European University Share Company
Nádor utca 11, H-1051 Budapest, Hungary
Tel: +36-1-327-3138 or 327-3000
Fax: +36-1-327-3183
E-mail: ceupress@ceu.hu
Website: www.ceupress.com

400 West 59th Street, New York NY 10019, USA
Tel: +1-212-547-6932
Fax: +1-212-548-4607
E-mail: mgreenwald@sorosny.org

ISBN 963 9241 94 6 cloth
ISBN 963 9241 93 8 paperback

Library of Congress Cataloging-in-Publication Data

Krastev, Ivan.
  Shifting obsessions : three essays on the politics of anticorruption / by
Ivan Krastev ; with a foreword by Aryeh Neier.
    p. cm.
  Includes bibliographical references and index.
  ISBN 9639241938 (hardbound) — ISBN 9639241946 (pbk.)
  1. Political corruption. 2. Political corruption—Prevention. 3. Political
corruption—Government policy., I. Title.

JF1081.K69 2004
364.1'323—dc22

                                    2004010839

Printed in Hungary by
Akadémiai Nyomda, Martonvásár

Table of Contents

List of Figures

Foreword

IN THE COURSE of a little more than a decade, the issue of corruption has become a leading focus of pubic policy-making worldwide. Previously, corruption was looked upon as an unfortunate but more or less inevitable by-product of human cunning, malevolence and frailty. It was the stuff of scandal. From time to time, it became the target of populist political campaigns but it was not previously regarded as the proper object of the deliberations and programs of important institutions. Today, however, corruption figures significantly in the policies and programs of a host of international bodies such as the World Bank, the International Monetary Fund and the World Trade Organization; it is a topic to be addressed seriously when world leaders gather, as at G-8 meetings; it is a growing factor in bilateral relations between states and special programs, such as America's Millennium Challenge Account, are explicitly designed to reward governments that have designed and implemented effective anticorruption strategies; a great many nongovernmental organizations operating internationally, or on a national or local basis in all parts of the world, have been formed specifically to address the problem of corruption or have altered their agendas to make it central to their work; it is the subject of a rapidly growing body of academic literature; and enough ordinary citizens have become engaged in campaigns to do something about the problem so that it is possible to discern the beginning of the formation of an "anticorruption movement" much as such other citizens movements—"the women's movement," "the human rights movement" and "the environmental movement"—emerged in the 1970s. The anticorruption cause is the first that is global in character since those others caught fire more than two decades earlier—other than the much looser and more chaotic anti-globalization effort—that may warrant the label of a movement.

The essays that are collected here are out of step with the general enthusiastic response to the sudden rise of the anticorruption cause. Though far from offering apologies for those who misuse public power and the public purse, they reflect more skepticism and wariness than we are accustomed to seeing. The motives and consequences of raising concerns about corruption, the authors suggest, may have a number of dimensions. It is not always possible to reduce the struggle over corruption to a simple question of doing evil versus doing good. For one thing, not all charges of corruption are well-founded. There may be demagogic components to such allegations. Labeling one's antagonists as corrupt may delegitimize them and make it difficult for them to defend themselves. Proving that one is not corrupt is not a simple matter.

Broad programs to control corruption by international financial institutions may also serve purposes that are not explicitly articulated. They can be a way for such bodies to assert their authority over client states and, in the process, to legitimize policies such as structural adjustment for which they have been the targets of much criticism both from populist antiglobalization forces and from some dissident economists. Most dangerously, the anticorruption cause can be a way for an authoritarian leader, such as a Vladimir Putin, to eliminate those he sees as challenging or obstructing his consolidation of power.

I am among those who believe that the current international preoccupation with corruption is a welcome and very healthy development. I am especially enthusiastic about the efforts of a group such as Global Witness that have called attention to the misuse of the funds that governments that control extensive natural resources, such as oil, gems and timber, have made from the income they derive from the extractive industries. The manner in which this corruption contributes not only to poor economic development and bad governance but also to severe human rights abuses and to prolonged and devastating armed conflict makes it urgent to address the problem through the combined efforts of nongovernmental groups, bilateral governmental relations and the international financial institutions. It is the citizens of countries afflicted by the "resource curse" who are the principal victims of corrupt practices by their own governments and by multinational corporations that collaborate with officials of those governments by failing to disclose the payments they make to harvest natural resources. Yet it is useful and sobering to be reminded that many a good cause attracts those who wish to exploit it for their own purposes, and that it may be put to bad uses. The anticorruption cause is no exception.

My hope is that these thoughtful and provocative essays will stimulate reflection and debate among the protagonists of the anticorruption movement. They could help those committed to that movement in good faith to pursue their cause more wisely, and in less of a spirit of self-rightcousness, than is often the case.

ARYEH NEIER

Preface

THERE ARE STRANGE functional similarities among the three discourses that largely shape global politics today—antiterrorism, anticorruption, and anti-Americanism. All three of them flourish at the end of history, when no universal alternative to democracy and the market is in play, but disappointment with democracy and the market is growing. Today democracy may often be redefined or distorted but it is not openly opposed. Anti-market and anti-capitalist sentiments are enjoying a subterranean resurgence, but on the surface they take the form of a debate between Joseph Stiglitz and the International Monetary Fund (IMF). What used to be a class struggle has now been reduced to a quarrel in the faculty lounge. The three dominant discourses are "empty boxes," easily filled with vague anxieties and cynically designed political strategies; each is a response to the growing gap between voting publics and their democratically elected elites. All three discourses can be used to criticize the status quo without incurring the odium of openly attacking democracy or the market. Groups with totally conflicting purposes can exploit all three to serve their own agendas.

When anticorruption rhetoric burst upon the stage of global politics in the early 1990s, it was conceptualized as a way to mobilize support for deepening market and democratic reforms. Anticorruption campaigns were designed as a coordinated effort by civil society and the international community (the World Bank, the IMF, and Western governments) to pressure national governments into delivering good governance. The anticorruption rhetoric shared by Washington and local civil society actors was intended to answer the question of what had gone wrong. Mass publics were ready to sign on. But the result has been that political competition in many democracies is now reduced to a confrontation between a government accused of corruption and an opposition that claims to be slightly less corrupt. Anticorruption campaigns have undermined politics understood as a matter of representative government and clashing ideas and programs. Far from contributing to a narrowing of the gap between publics and elites, anticorruption discourse has enlarged the gap.

When terrorism captured the global imagination after 9/11, antiterrorist discourse was designed to highlight the common threat that would help shore up the new world order. In fact, however, various governments have hijacked the antiterrorist agenda in order to destroy their local political opposition and to gain control over civil society. Antiterrorist discourse has been skillfully used to foster suspicion of NGOs and independent media and to curb civil liberties. Governments seized the opportunity and started manufacturing terrorists. A successful mixture of antiterrorist and anticorruption rhetoric, moderate anti-Americanism, and old-style administrative politics has enabled Vladimir Putin to consolidate an "acceptable" authoritarian regime in Russia. This model has the potential to be replicated. Governments that had found their freedom of action modestly weakened by the spread of democracy and global interdependence have used antiterrorism to bolster their control and enhance the secrecy of their operations.

The impact of anti-American discourse is likely to be similarly harmful to democracy. Washington adopted a high profile in promoting the anticorruption agenda, attempting to bypass governments by telling civil society actors that corrupt governments are the problem. In the case of antiterrorism, Washington allowed discredited governments to label their domestic opponents as terrorists in return for support in the global "war on terrorism." In the case of anti-Americanism, governments are trying to convince frustrated publics that America is the problem. The anticorruption drive was designed to promote the spread of capitalism and deepen democracy. Currently it fails. These three essays are three modest attempts to explain why the failure was to be expected.

Acknowledgements

TRAVELING IN THE LANDS of anti-corruption rhetoric and anti-corruption politics resembles the world of real corruption in one critical aspect: one person is not enough. In order to practice corruption or to study it, you need a partner. Different people and institutions made this tiny book possible. They did not simply contribute to the book, they are part of it. I was lucky to start my work on corruption in the Wissenschaftskolleg in Berlin—a place, where ideas and people meet like in few other places in the world. My colleagues there always asked me unexpected and sharp questions and they did not tolerate trivial answers—a dream start for a new project. Shalini Randeria deserves special mentioning for her generous comments and interest in my work. The idea of this book traveled with me to the Woodrow Wilson International Center for Scholars in Washington D.C. and to the Institute for Human Sciences in Vienna. Professor Lidia Basta and the Institute of Federalism at the University of Fribourg not simply hosted my obsessive interest in anti-corruption politics for a while but even encouraged them. My participation in the focus group on "Honesty and Trust" in Collegium Budapest led by János Kornai and Susan Rose-Ackerman were critical for the shaping of the book.

Professor Stephen Holmes from NYU and Thomas Carothers from Carnegie Endowment also could not escape my gratitude. It is also difficult to find the place of Open Society Institute on my map of gratitude, but without the spirit of open society and keen interest in the unintended consequences this work would not be the same.

But there are three partners without whom this book was never to be born. Yehuda Elkana, who encouraged me to go through with my argument; my family and especially my wife, who for several years were forced to live with my anticorruption obsessions without complaining; and my colleagues from CLS (Centre for Liberal Strategies, Sofia, Dr. Georgy Ganev in particular), who were the only ones capable to moderate the shiftings of my obsessions. These last three are my partners in the crime of writing this book.

April 7, 2004

When "Should" Does Not Imply "Can." The Making of the Washington Consensus on Corruption*

> "God does not take shohadh (bribes)"
> The Book of Deuteronomy

" GOING BEYOND THE DATA—wrote John T. Noonan, Jr—I venture a prediction: as slavery was once a way of life and now has become obsolete and incomprehensible, so the practice of bribery will become obsolete" (John T. Noonan, Jr, 1984). This prophecy, made almost two decades ago by the pre-eminent American moralist and expert on bribe, in a sense has turned out to be correct. The practice of bribery in fact has not become so obsolete as slavery, just on the contrary, it has become as widespread as McDonalds, but the anticorruption rhetoric has started to resemble the anti-slavery rhetoric. World leaders, journalists and ordinary citizens became simply obsessed with corruption. Asked to justify the policy of structural adjustments promoted by the IMF, Michael Camdessus answered that the IMF-backed restriction policies have their

* I would like to thank my Agora co-fellows for the pleasure of working together, and I am especially grateful to Shalini Randeria for coining the term "Washington consensus on corruption." It was such an important phrase that I decided to put it in the subtitle.

1

almost religious justification. "You cannot denounce the structural adjustments and be against the structure of the sin—proclaimed Camdessus. If you are against the structures of the sin that plague our world —corruption, nepotism, collusion, protectionism— you must go for structural adjustment, like it or not."[1]

The divine paradigm, structural adjustment and democracy are mysteriously mixed in the modern anticorruption fairy tale. The new anticorruption consensus is the vital point where the agenda of democratization and the agenda of free market meet, the point at which the global elites meet the demand of the local democratic publics. The story of the making of the anticorruption consensus is the story of how globalization works. It is a story of the happy marriage of "global" and "local," where the "global" are the International Financial Institutions, Western governments, international media and the multinational corporations, and the "local" are the civic groups, local media and reform-minded politicians.

My study presses the question how the global consensus on corruption became possible. What is its content? And what is its future? It is not a study of the anticorruption policies. It is a study in the politics of anticorruption. The study of policies is a study of what institutions did and do. The study of politics

---

1. Interview with Michel Camdessus, Foreign Policy, September–October, 2000.

is a study of why they did or do it. And it is the "why" and not the "what" that interests me.

The study is focused on strategies and inter-relations of the leading global players in the politics of anticorruption—IMF and World Bank, the leading multinational companies and Transparency International as the leading global NGO involved in the anticorruption business. In telling the story how corruption was constructed as a global policy issue and how the global policy response to corruption was designed, this chapter is structured in four parts.

The first part examines why corruption became a global concern. The second part focuses on why corruption became the concern of the institutions of the Washington consensus. The third part explains how the new science on corruption came into being

A conclusion demonstrates the complex nature of the tradeoffs between global and local in sustaining the anticorruption consensus and reflects on the uneasy relationship between anticorruption and reform.

Starting a research on corruption is such an obvious choice for an East European political scientist that I feel obliged to excuse myself. It was not corruption that captured my imagination. It was the way corruption is debated today that struck me more than corruption itself. I decided to study not the "banality of evil"-corruption, but the ambiguity of the benevolent anticorruption crusade.

For years corruption was one discourse that always demanded stories. Numbers alone did not excite imagination. Most people sensed that there was no such thing as an objective social science about corruption. Corruption was one science where every victim felt expert. Corruption discourse was about juicy details, names, places, and conspiratorial fantasies. Corruption was seen as sleazy, ambiguous and impossible to be put into meaningful mathematical models. Corruption like cooking and gardening was recognized to be a subject in the kingdom of local knowledge. People were usually skeptical about chances to fight corruption. Anticorruption campaigns have always been viewed with enthusiasm in the beginning and cynicism in the end (Visvanatan and Sethi, 1998).

All that is not true any more. Corruption—a realm of anthropologists, sociologists and political scientists—was conquered by economists. A global World Bank led anticorruption campaign is under way, and almost nobody dares to be skeptical about it.

Anticorruption consensus claims to bridge the distinctions between left and right, liberal and conservative, globalization and anti-globalization. In comparison with the other features of the global age-free trade, information revolution and even the introduction of universal human rights standards, the global policy response to corruption is the least contested. In the days when activists are storming the streets of Seattle and Prague protesting against the social costs of globalization, anticorruption policies remained the only sphere where the consensus between global and local, left and right is still intact. Local NGOs and pro-democracy groups actively cooperate with World Bank to curb corruption.[2] They view foreign investors

4

and foreign governments as allies and not as enemies. But does that mean that local civic groups have agreed with Camdessus that in order to fight the structure of sin, you should endorse structural adjustments, like it or not? Is the anticorruption consensus a consensus on the policy response to corruption?

Why Corruption Became a Global Concern

The last decade of the 20th century is remarkable for the global explosion of the interest in corruption. In the years 1982–1987, the word corruption appeared in average 229 times a year on the pages of The Economist and Financial Times. In the period 1989–1992, corruption appeared in average 502 times a year. In 1993 the word corruption was mentioned 1076 times in the two most respected European publications on politics and finance. In 1994 corruption was mentioned 1099 times, in 1995, 1246 times. And this tendency sustains till now.

But the popularity of corruption is not limited to books. IMF and World Bank included transparency clauses in their loan giving practices. In 1996 World Bank revised its guidelines to state explicitly that corruption and fraud would be grounds for canceling the contract if the borrower has not taken appropriate ac-

---

2. For more on this cooperation see
               www.worldbank.org/wbi/governance.

tion. In December 1997 the Council of OECD signed an international convention that requires signatories to outlaw overseas bribery of foreign officials. In 1997 IMF suspended 227 million dollars loan to Kenya because of bad governance concerns. 1997 World Bank and IMF annual meeting had a special focus on corruption. Billions of dollars were spent in the last five years on anticorruption projects. Corruption hit the top of the political agenda in countries as different as Russia, China, US, Germany, Mexico and Nigeria.

What has happened? Do we have more corruption today? Do we have a more harmful corruption? Why the global world became less tolerant to it than our pre-global world was?

The fast growing literature on corruption (Tanzi, 1998; Rose-Ackerman, 1999) suggests several basic directions in answering these questions.

The End of the Cold War. The end of the Cold war put an end to a period of political hypocrisy. There was no reason any more for Western democracies to support corrupt dictators. When Soviet threat was removed the corruption ceased to be a security issue.

The end of the cold war was also the end of the great ideological confrontation inside the developed and developing countries. Explaining the success of the operation "Clean hands" in Italy Romano Prodi used only one word—"Yalta." The end of Yalta convinced Italian businesses that paying the "party tax" was not legitimate any more.

The End of Ideology. The end of communism challenged the very legitimacy of democracy. Deprived of the great ideological clash, citizens in the Western democracies focused their attention on the integrity and personality of people in politics. "Americanization" of the European politics replaced the old economy of "selling ideology" with the new economy of "selling leaders." Moral values and personal integrity of the politicians captured the imagination of the publics.

The End of Real Socialism. In Eastern Europe the new anticorruption sensitivity has specific sources. The old system of exchanges of favors that was typical and massively spread in the communist period was replaced by less sophisticated bribery. Eastern Europe made transition from "give me a favor society" into "give me a bribe society."

The eruption of social inequality that took place in post-communist countries was difficult to be explained in the terms of entrepreneurship and hard working. The emergence of new rich and new poor and the unexplained circumstances of success and failure made people to believe that corruption was the only credible explanation. Massive privatization was the other critical factor increasing the incentives for corrupt behavior. It is enough to imagine the scale of re-distribution of wealth taking place in the former Soviet block in order to understand Eastern Europe's fixation with corruption (World Bank, 2000).

The Rise of the New Media. The new global information environment and the popularity of the investigative journalism are the other factors contributing to the new visibility of corruption. Today just by click of the mouse people can learn about the Kohl Affair in Germany, Kremlin credit card scandal and the scandal with the Bank of New York. Corruption sells well, because bribe is "as intimate as a seduction and as coercive as a rape." Publishing corruption stories pays as nicely as investing into Internet stock and the risk is lower.

The Rise of Democracy. The spread of democracy is also part of the explanation why corruption became so debated. Democracies are not by definition clearer than the non-democratic regimes, but in democratic countries governments go to ballot boxes and even risk not to be re-elected. The electoral competition increases the probability that acts of corruption would come to the surface. The fact that more countries are going to the polls made corruption more visible and important in a global scale.

The Rise of the Global Market. The new mobility and the new global market also contributed to corruption's visibility. In the words of Vito Tanzi "globalization has brought individuals from countries with little corruption into frequent contacts with those from countries where corruption is endemic. These contacts have increased the international attention paid to corruption, especially when some companies believed that they were cut out of some contracts because the winning company has paid a bribe" (Tanzi, 1998).

The Rise of Civil Society. The rise of the civil society and the public awareness campaigns arranged by NGOs mobilized significant anticorruption sentiments. Civic advocacy is partially responsible for making corruption not simply the problem of the corrupted countries but also a problem for countries and foreign companies corrupting them. It was civil activists that focus attention on the fact that corruption money earned in the East is kept in the banks of the West.

The Rise of Organized Crime. The Interpol reports that only for the year 1999 the estimated profit of the organized crime is between 400 billion dollars and 650 billion dollars. In the language of the political science corruption and organized crime are structurally connected. Corruption weakens the state preventing it from being effective third party. The failure of state to enforce rules creates a vacuum to be filled by the organized crime. When the government and the judicial system are so corrupted that they cannot help the contract to be enforced, the only available enforcer is the Mafia. In this respect organized crime is viewed both as a source and product of rising corruption.

"This, that and the other" factors have been used to explain corruption's new visibility. They illustrate the urgency with which corruption has become a global concern. But all these factors are still insufficient to explain how corruption was turned into a global policy issue, and why the World Bank and IMF addressed it as one of the structures of economic sin.

The dozens of corruption scandals that erupted in the last decade are not very different from the waves of scandals in the past. It is enough to recall the corrupted 1970s with Watergate and the famous Lockheed scandal. It is enough to recall the Flick-affair in Germany and serial scandals that have broken in Latin America. In all cold war years corruption was a major issue with respect to developing countries, and media was investigating it intensively.

But nevertheless that corruption was a major concern before it was a non-issue in the field of international politics. Why it is an issue now? Has corruption increased or has the world changed?

The current anticorruption literature assumes that the new interest in corruption is a result either of the increase of corruption or of the increase of corruption visibility. It starts with the fact that the new global anticorruption consensus is a response to changes in the field of corruption or its perception. My hypothesis is the reverse one. It was the new anticorruption rhetoric that came as a response to changes in the politics of international trade and the politics of International Financial Institutions that resulted in the new visibility of corruption and the new conceptualization of its role. It was not the reality of "more corruption" that produced the global anticorruption response. It was the promotion of centrality of corruption as a policy problem that brought the data of more corruption. It is the story of the making of the global anticorruption consensus much more than the study of corruption per se that gives us an insight in the kitchen of globalization. The study of the new anticorruption consensus should not be reduced to the study of how corruption "was discovered" as a major policy issue. It makes sense to study also who "has discovered it" and why.

Why Corruption was Discovered as a Global Issue

The popularized story of how the World Bank, IMF and OECD have discovered corruption and decided to fight it reads like a civil society soup opera. In this popular version the new global response on corruption came as a result of the pressure coming from the democratic publics. It was the newly emerging global civil society pushing for global anticorruption policy.

This story tells that in the beginning was Transparency International. It was founded in 1993 by a group of former World Bank executives[3] and dedicated itself to fighting corruption and promoting transparency around the world. In a few years TI made a difference. It was pressure coming from TI that urged

---

3. More on Transparancy International on
www.transparency.de.

11

the international organizations to realize that corruption is a global problem that cannot be located in the Third World and Eastern Europe. The manner in which OECD countries treated corruption outside their borders was made responsible for the present "corruption epidemic." It was this dissident message coming from TI that changed the established views on corruption. In the next part of my study I will concentrate on how TI got its message through. But now I want to stress the fact that anticorruption strategy adopted by TI was essential for building a broad coalition. TI refused to deal with concrete cases of corruption and concentrated its efforts on advocating institutional changes. The anticorruption discourse adopted by TI was not the muckraking discourse of the local anticorruption activists, it was the discourse of the reformers inside the international institutions. It was not about combating corruption. It was about introducing transparency. The non-confrontational approach in fighting corruption was re-enforced by the very organizational structure of TI. Its national chapters have brought together the representatives of the civic community, business and government, and the national chapters remain autonomous in the framework of the global TI. This corporate approach in mobilizing support for anticorruption policies turned out to be very successful in dealing with international institutions, but it remained distanced from the local anticorruption debates. The names of notorious heroes of the local corruption scandals can be often found among the founders of the national chapters of TI. TI is so inclusive in its approach that it is often difficult to figure out its opponents. But in the civil society version of the present outburst of honesty it was TI that produced the change.

Readings of the archives of the current anticorruption revolution suggest some other answers to the question how corruption became a global issue. TI can be seen as a factor for creating the present anticorruption consensus, but it can be viewed also as an instrument of a policy that was already agreed in World Bank and US State Department.

The US against Corruption

In this alternative story in the beginning was not Transparency International but the US State Department. In the words of Patrick Glynn, Stephen Korbin and Moises Naim "a major shift in American policy on bribery question came after the trade minded Clinton administration assumed office in 1993. Departing from their predecessors' back-burner approach, Secretary of State Warren Christopher and Assistant Secretary of State for Economic and Business Affairs Daniel Tarullo decided to make the OECD bribery negotiation a State Department priority. Both reflected the long dominant wish in the American business community for a level playing field" (Kimberly Ann Elliot, 1997). The obsession of the American business community with corruption has its history in 1970s. The post-Watergate spirit of "soul searching" and the shock of the Lockheed scandal pushed American legislators to introduce in 1977 the Foreign Corruption Practices Act (amended in 1988) that criminalized the bribery of foreign officials by American citizens and companies. Starting with 1970s American business community complained that US's tougher position on corruption significantly affects the trade opportunities of American companies working in the bribe-expecting environments of the Third world. A 1996 Commerce Department report prepared with the assistance of the US intelligence agencies estimated that American firms have lost 11 billion dollars worth of business for the years 1994 and 1995 to competitors that paid bribes. The Economist quotes another governmental study that claimed that in 1994 and 1995 American firms lost some 100 deals worth 45 billion dollars to less principled rivals. The underlying analyses remained classified. It is difficult to know how the losses were estimated. But on the base of such figures US started its campaign to press the other OECD countries to criminalize payment of bribes to foreign officials and change the rules that make bribes tax deductible in countries like Germany and France. Major factor in US's policy in the area of bribe negotiations was the public pressure on European governments. "The embarrassing factor in these negotiations was very high"—confessed one of the European negotiators.

The trade version of the discovery of corruption shows that the discovery of corruption as a global policy issue can not be reduced to the fashionable "pressure from below." It was much more a combination of pressure from below and pressure from US in which both sides used and misused each other in the global anticorruption dance.

And there were at least two other global players that had good and very specific reasons to change their attitude with respect to corruption—multinational companies and Breton woods institutions.

Multinationals against Corruption

In the traditional perception of corruption, the "conversion" of multinational companies from sources of corruption into fighters against corruption is a dramatic change. To illustrate the extent to which foreign capital was once seen as a source of corruption we have only to point out that in the Bulgarian language, all French, German, and English words for doing business have the connotation of performing a corrupt act.

In 1960 and 1970s, foreign investors considered corruption to be a useful vehicle for opening up and modernizing the economies of developing countries. Corruption was an instrument to break the official protectionist barriers that were imposed by the governments of the post-colonial states.

In the brave new WTO world protectionism is an unaffordable luxury for most governments. In the transition economies of Central and Eastern Europe, protectionism is simply unthinkable. Their dependency on IMF loans and their competition for foreign direct investments has forced them to open their economies and to adopt non-protectionist legislation. This new open environment is the major reason for multinationals' change of mind with respect to corruption.

Compared with the normal markets of goods and services, corrupted markets are characterized by the very high value of the local knowledge. In order to corrupt public officials and to win the contract one cannot rely simply on offering the biggest bribe in the biggest brown-paper bag. The market in corruption services is a clandestine, closed market. In order to be competitive on this market, one has to know when, to whom and how to give a bribe. Local businesses are much better positioned in the corruption market because they are plugged in the existing networks and because they posses local knowledge. In other words, corrupted business environment is much more favorable to local businesses than to foreign investors. The great corruption scandals in Eastern Europe in the last years are not scandals of multinationals winning contracts, they are scandals of multinationals loosing contracts or seeing their property rights undermined. The story of the velvet take over of the Russian oil company Yukos by the oligarch Mihail Khodorkovsky in the framework of the loan-for-shares scheme in 1996 is the classical illustration of the "corruption as protectionism" thesis. In her insightful book "Sale of the Century" (Freeland, 2000) Chrystia Feeland, the Financial Times correspondent in Moscow between

January 1995 and August 1998 reveals the secret story of the deal. In the beginning Khodorkovsky reached an agreement with the other Russian oligarchs that Yukos "belongs" to him. His next task was to keep foreigners out. Yukos had been classed as a "strategic company" which means that foreigners were officially banned from buying, but Khodorkovsky worried that might not be enough. Outsiders might try to find loopholes in the law, perhaps by acting in concert with a Russian company. Khodorkovsky did everything necessary to neutralize the threat. Menatep (his group) launched an intense legal and political campaign. Konstantin Kagalovsky (Russia's ex-representative to the IMF and mastermind of the campaign) few years later explained to Freeland the technique for keeping the foreigners out. The key, he said was to ensure that the law banning foreign participation was intentionally vague and thus open to interpretations. If the foreign firms did decide to try to find a legal loophole and make a bid for Yukos through Russian partners, Kagalovsky would warn them that Menatep would take them to court. With the law so open to interpretations, and the home court advantage, Menatep would stand a strong chance of winning.

The whole point was to transform the decision for foreign firms from a purely legal question—Could they find a legal technicality that would permit them to participate in loans-for-shares?—into a political one—Did they have the domestic connections and savvy to outfox a powerful Russian company in a battle waged in the murky swamp of Russian legislation?

"When the laws are unclear, then you can not simply hire lawyers (and have them decide the issue)— Kagalovsky explained.—You have to decide yourself whether you are willing to run the risk."

This was an impressively devious scheme and it worked. Foreign firms were unwilling to run the risk. But Chrystia Freeland was intrigued how had Kagalovsky ensured that the laws were written in so precisely vague a fashion as to make it legally too risky for foreigners to participate. Kagalovsky's answer was an enlightening one "Well, of course, I wrote the law myself, and I took special care with it."

The notorious vagueness of the Russian laws turned out to be not the result of the terrible Russian/Soviet legacy, not result of bad foreign advice, but something totally different. The laws were vague on purpose and their explicit goal was to keep foreigners out. The Byzantine story of the "purchase" of Yukos is the best illustration of the fact that only insiders survive in the oil fields of Siberia.

In a private conversation a senior British diplomat complained that Western investors are simply not allowed to enter the corrupt market. "They simply do not want us—said the diplomat—they do not want our investments, they do not want even our bribes."[4]

It was the discovery that corruption is a hidden form of protectionism that is mainly responsible for multinationals joining the anticorruption movement

---

4. Interview of the author of this essay.

18

and pressing for effective curbing of corruption. It does not mean that multinationals are not corrupting any more, it simply means that now they prefer the normal markets. In comparison with the developing world where multinationals—especially those tied with the former colonizers—are "local" and enjoy the fact that they are plugged in the existing networks, in the former Soviet block foreign investors discovered the price of being outsider.

World Bank against Corruption

But it was not only multinationals and US that discovered that corruption is disadvantageous, it was the World Bank and (by association) IMF that discovered that corruption can be useful in solving other problems.

It tends to be forgotten that both World Bank and IMF were Cold war institutions and that their missions have been shaped in the context of the global confrontation between the free world and communism. World Bank played an important role in preventing the invasion of communism in the poor third world countries. In playing its assisting but also containing role, the World Bank was particularly cautious with the sensitivities of its third world clients. For the whole cold war period the word "corruption" was simply absent from the vocabulary of the IMF and the World Bank. "When I came to the World Bank—wrote James Wolfensohn—I was told that there was one word I could not use, which was the 'C' word, the 'C' word being 'corruption'. Corruption, you see, was identified with politics, and if I got into that, I would have a terrible time with my Board."[5]

But starting with 1996 World Bank and IMF were not in a position to keep corruption out of their concern. Several reasons are responsible for the World Bank and IMF turning face to corruption. The first reason was the pressure for more transparency and accountability with respect to World Bank and IMF programs. In the eyes of its critics the institutions of Washington consensus were not just soft on corruption, they were blamed for being sources of corruption. The second reason was the US pressure to include good governance as part of the World Bank and IMF conditionalities. The third was the escalating criticism of the policies of the Washington consensus, especially with respect to IMF and the World Bank performance in Russia, and pressure from influential conservative circles in US to close the World Bank or at least to minimize its role (Naim Moises, 2000).

Fighting corruption became part of the new strategy of the World Bank and to a lesser extent of IMF to prove their usefulness in the post-cold war world.

For the Bank, the agenda of good governance and transparency made three distinctive gains: it put in one package the management re-structuring of the institution, undertaken by the new president James

---

5. Remarks at Global Forum on Fighting Corruption.

Wolfensohn, and the new stress on institution-building and knowledge; it improved the image of the Bank; and thirdly, it allowed the Bank to distinguish itself from the orthodox policies of the IMF.

In its 1997 Report the Bank re-discovered the state and reformulated its position on the relations between the state and the market. The conclusion of the Bank was that functioning market is impossible in the absence of the functioning state and that institutional reforms should be the priority in the process of transition.

It was not the wrong policies but the wrong priorities that were blamed for the policy failures. In the vocabulary of the Washington consensus the weak institutional environment was responsible for the failure of the initial reform package in places like Russia. Corruption served the role of a general explanation for a variety of policies failures in different environments. What constituted a common place between the different cases of failure was the existence of endemic corruption. Focus on corruption helped the Bank to explain its failures. It also gave a platform for in-house reformers like Joseph Stiglitz to ask for the change in the orthodoxy. But in order to address corruption, the World Bank needed to de-politicize it. "I visited a number of countries—recalled Wolfensohn—and I decided that I would redefine the 'C' word not as a political issue but as something social and economic." The redefinition took place in 1996. Corruption was not about politics any more.

The success of the second-generation reforms was

declared conditional on the successful elimination of hyper-corruption. There was a need for comprehensive global anticorruption initiative. In 1997 the World Bank published a policy document entitled "Helping Countries Combat Corruption" that placed the World Bank as an anticorruption advisor of last resort.

At the same time it is important to underline that World Bank's "discovery" of corruption can not be reduced to a cynical strategy designed to recycle old policies and to gain new legitimacy. Such an interpretation is close to the heart of the radical leftists and to the radical French, but it misses an important point. It was the emergence of the World Bank's experience with Russia as the paradigm-maker in reformulating the problems of global development that explains the new anticorruption obsession of the International Financial Institutions. The obsession with corruption was the direct result from the obsession with Russia and transition economies as whole.

How the New Science of Corruption Was Born

This most intriguing part of my story is not about the American pressure on OECD negotiations on bribery, it is not on the World Bank's obsession with Russia and its institutional interest in turning corruption into an economic issue. It is not a story about the role of the global NGOs. It is a story about social sciences.

The invention of corruption as a global policy issue that can be solved with the "one size fits all" policy would be unimaginable without the radical discovery that corruption is measurable. It was the radical transformation of the social sciences' discourse on corruption that made the current global anticorruption campaign possible. The new anticorruption consensus brought into life the new anticorruption science. And the new anticorruption science manufactured the data that have justified the new anticorruption consensus.

Corruption was traditionally a strange issue for the social sciences. It is almost absent from the theoretical discourse in the end of 19th and the beginning of 20th century. "Corruption" is absent in the indexes of the collected volumes of Marx and Mill. For the 19th century corruption was something to live with, something to gossip about, and something to complain against, but not something to reflect upon. "Corruption" could be found in the newspapers and pamphlets but not in the scholars' works.

It was the perception of corruption mainly as a moral issue that kept it out of the interest of social researchers. In his book "Corruption: Ethics and Power in Florence in 1600–1770" Jean-Claude Waquet shows that in the studied period the discourse on corruption was not a discourse on government but a discourse on human nature. This is the reason why corruption was reported but not reflected in the political literature. The conviction of moderns that corrupted individuals corrupt institutions made corruption marginal to the debate on institutions. The successful anticorruption reforms that were undertaken in US in the late 19th century came more as a result of two distinctive organizational dysfunctions than as a result of the new ideas in studying corruption. It was the growing ineffectiveness of contracting out public services and the growing inefficiency of patronage-based employment as government grew up, that created a momentum for civil service reform (Ackerman, 1999).

In recent times the uneasiness of social sciences with corruption is related to the problem of definition. Definition that is universal enough to include all the acts of corruption in different cultures and different historical times, and a definition that will turn the debate on corruption in something more than a serial of case studies.

Three basic approaches are competing in defining political corruption. The first defines it as an abuse of public office for private gains. The second defines corruption with respect to public interest and public opinion. And the third is a market-centered definition, where corruption is defined as market type of behavior outside the realm of the market. All these definitions have their strong and weak points. And they all define in a different way what we study when we study corruption (Heywood, 1997). The definition debate was constantly coming back confronted with questions like: can we confine our research on corruption to the acts of misuse of public office that are criminalized by the law, or should we also include the acts of corruption that are still not criminalized. How should we treat the situation when certain acts are perceived as corrupt by the existing colonial legislation, but public opinion does not perceive them as corruption? And if we adopt public interest or public opinion centered definitions of corruption, how to define the public interest, and whose opinion is public opinion? Should we confine corruption to its monetary forms or should we include also the non-monetary forms of bribery? How private gain should be defined in the context of corruption research? All these discussions are well known to scholars of corruption.

But the major problem about corruption never really was how to agree on a working definition: the problem was the data. Because corruption is a crime but it is a crime that nobody is interested to report, the cases of corruption ending in court are insignificant in comparison with the number of corruption transactions taking place. And the proven cases of corruption are ridiculously rare. Reliance on public opinion can be also misleading. Anticorruption rhetoric is often used for political purposes and the conviction of the public that their or their neighbor's society is corrupted register more often the prevailing of anticorruption rhetoric than the actual state of affairs.

The problem of data is also the problem of the legitimacy in measuring corruption. What do we claim when we say that corruption has increased in a certain country? Do we claim that there are more corrupt transactions per person, do we claim that more people are involved in acts of corruption, do we claim that public opinion perceives the country as more corrupt, or do we claim that corruption has reached the highest levels of power?

The other difficulty with corruption is defining its functions in society. The present consensus that corruption hurts development was not a common sense even a decade ago. In the 1960s and 1970s corruption was an excessively debated issue with respect to the Third World but there was no consensus on its effects on development. The economic miracle in Asia did not support hard stand on corruption. South East Asian tigers did well despite the fact that they were perceived as corrupt. The other reason making scholars and policy-makers cautious in condemning corruption was political. In the cold war period corruption was viewed by many as a democratic disease: so many military coups and communist takeovers in different parts of the world were legitimized with anticorruption rhetoric. "Graft is a factor in the Cold war"—wrote *The Economist* in 1957. The anticorruption rhetoric was perceived as the cover for communist revolutionary rhetoric.

In the 1960s and 1970s there were two principal schools in assessing the role of corruption in developing countries. In the view of people like Huntington corruption could have positive effects. It reduced violence. And was a form of adjustment to modernization. It was anti-revolutionary. "He who corrupts a system's police officer—claimed Huntington—is more likely to identify with the system than he who storms the system's police station" (Huntington, 1968).

Corruption apologists adopted Robert Merton's functionalist analysis of the political machines in the US in showing that corruption can not be analyzed outside the concrete context in which it appears and that in many cases corruption is functional for the development of society.

In his book "Comparative Political Corruption" James Scott demonstrated several hidden functions of corruption in the context of post-colonial modernization. Corruption, for example, was the only channel for Chinese minority in Malaysia to have access to the political decision-making. In the case of Soviet Union *"blat"* (non-monetary exchange of favors) was perceived as a form of adjustment of the population to the economy of shortages. In the late 1964, Nathaniel Leff of Columbia University argued that "corruption may introduce an element of competition into what is otherwise a comfortably monopolistic industry...and tendency towards efficiency can be introduced into the system" (Leff, 1964). Bribery was also rationalized as time saving mechanism for transactions taking place in highly bureaucratic environments.

The moralizing school in debating corruption was not ready to accept the progressive role of bribe in the developing countries. It pointed to the lasting effect of corruption on the functioning of the national administration and its negative effect on civic culture. Corruption critics estimated the effects of corruption much more in the long perspective of state and society building than in the perspective of its immediate costs. But what was common place between apologists and moralizers was the understanding that corruption is a context sensitive issue, and that analysis of corruption should be contextual in its nature. It was a heresy in the 1960s and 1970s to believe that a global anticorruption policy package can be designed and that it can be offered to Nigeria, Russia, Mexico and China at the same time.

In the context of this old debate the current anticorruption paradigm is distinctively new. The decontextualization of the anticorruption knowledge started with turning corruption from political into economic problem. Three major "discoveries" followed, that gave birth to the new anticorruption paradigm.

First was the discovery that corruption is an institutional problem. Second was the discovery that old knowledge on corruption is policy irrelevant. And finally the great discovery that corruption could be quantified.

The story of these three great discoveries is the story of how the economic discourse marginalized all other discourses in debating corruption. The major turn in understanding corruption was the assumption that the corruption act is a rational behavior that takes place under certain incentives. Putting incentives right was declared enough to reduce the endemic corruption behavior. If in the 17th century people tended to believe that corrupt people corrupt the institutions. The last years not simply demonstrated that institutions corrupt people, but insisted that the problem of corruption is the problem of policy choices. People are corrupted because they implement policies that sustain corruption. In its economic formulation the discourse on corruption is de-contextualized and normative. It is the individuals and not the community and its adopted practices that were turned into the only legitimate starting point in studying corruption.

This de-contextualization of the understanding of corruption became possible because non-economists failed to argue the risk of global anticorruption policy. The failure of the anthropologists, sociologists and political scientists to challenge economists' monopoly over the corruption debate has to do with the discovery of the political incorrectness of the cultural arguments with respect to corruption. In the development debate in the 1960s many anthropologists and political scientists focused their attention on the case studies of corruption, illustrating the fact that different forms of corruption characterize different political and cultural regimes. Differentiation was the basic methodology in studying corruption. The individual was "rationalized" in his/her own cultural and political environment. The old discourse on corruption was arguing that different political regimes create conditions for different type of corruption. No direct connection between the spread of the petty corruption and the rise of political corruption was found. The old discourse was looking for explanations. It was a corruption and not anticorruption discourse.

In arguing that Western norms for corrupt behavior are not applicable to the non-western societies, most of anthropologists and political scientists perceived their position as defense of non-western societies against the unfair accusations of them being over-corrupted. In the 1980s the same arguments for cultural distinctiveness started to be read as a pretext for treating these societies as inferior with respect to development and economic growth. Anthropologist found their position severely attacked by their beloved natives. The academic debate on the political economy of corruption in Africa in the last years illustrates the resistance of the Africans to study corruption in cultural terms. This opened room for global approach to the issues of corruption and fitted to the policies of the Washington consensus.

The Washington consensus that was the flavor of the 1980s marked the end of the split between the development economics and the mainstream economic theory. It was accepted that the way in which nations became prosperous is not different for the different parts of the world. Moreover, it was discovered that prosperity could be achieved simply by adopting the right policies and sticking to them.

This radical turn in understanding development reformulated the major findings of the old corruption studies. It was a commonplace in the 1960s that poorer countries tend to be more corrupted. In the 1990s the common sense was that it is not that poor countries are more corrupted, it was that corrupted countries are poor.

The claim of the new anticorruption science was that corruption has nothing to do with cultures, corruption is characteristic of institutional environments and characteristic of certain policies.

But all this new knowledge on corruption was normative in its nature. It was very difficult to verify it, because corruption was not measurable. Turning corruption into de-politicized economic issue needed new tools for studying it.

The new moment in constructing corruption as a global issue was the discovery that corruption can be measured.

Like all great discoveries, the discovery that corruption can be measured was a child of luck, interest and accident. In its willingness to influence the public and to mobilize support for global anticorruption actions Transparency International decided to produce a ranking of the countries according to the way their level of corruption is perceived by the senior executives of multinational companies. In 1994 TI produced its first corruption perception index.[6] Interviewing senior and experienced executives of multinational companies and balancing their answers with the information coming from other sources TI came with a table ranking 53 countries in the world. The impact of the corruption index was shattering. All

---

6. TI corruption perception indexes can be seen on
www.transparency.de.

major newspapers around the world published it and comment on it. Opposition parties started to refer to it. Governments began to attack it. But the most important effect was the public conviction that it was possible to compare how corrupt certain countries are and to monitor the rise of corruption in a single country.

The estimation of corruption on a national level was not an invention of TI: a company called Political Risk Services has been making for years its estimations of the corruptiveness of the business environment in different countries. It has been offering its estimations to business clients but these estimations were never presented as "measuring corruption." Political Risk Services kept its estimations private and never made a scientific claim with respect to its ranking. The company knew that its corruption estimations are based on impressionistic evidences.

Publicizing their corruption perception index, Transparency International also did not declare that they succeeded in measuring actual corruption. The expert part of the group underlined that this was perception index.[7] But the thing was done. The ranking was in the newspapers. The next stage was easy. When the ranking was produced econometrists started to work on this ranking, or the Political Risk Services ranking, producing cross-country regress analyses.

---

7. Over the years TI experts worked constantly on their methodology.

The list of findings reads like this: corruption hurts economic growth; it reduces the level of foreign investment, that is if two countries have otherwise equal conditions FDI will go to the less corrupted one; corruption hurts mostly poor people; it distorts the logic of public investment (governments favor projects with higher corruption potential), and so on (Tanzi, 1998; Rose-Ackerman, 1999).

Corruption was not any more about anecdotes and contextually sensitive analysis. The study of corruption was portrayed as similar to the study of inflation. The causes of corruption were reduced to the effect of the governments' role in politics. The Transparency International corruption index that was designed as a PR instrument was manipulatively turned into hard data on the base of which the new anticorruption policies started to be designed. Economists managed to solve the basic problem with respect to corruption —the lack of data, and on the base of the legitimacy enjoyed by any quantitative type of analysis radically marginalized non-economic discourses on corruption. Recently several researchers, including World Bank in-house researchers [8] criticized the methodology of Transparency International. They tried to put limits to the speculations coming from the quantitative analysis of corruption, but this clarification can not change the fact that the discovery of the measure-

---

8. Daniel Kaufman, www.worldbank.org/wbi/gac.

ment of corruption radically changed the discourse on it. The latest publications on the issue are full of statistical correlations.[9]

It was this major change in studying corruption that legitimized and made the new global anticorruption policy package possible.

Anticorruption and Reform

The study of the making of the anticorruption consensus contrary to the assumption of the current anticorruption studies makes me believe that the global anticorruption consensus was not the result or response to the rise in corruption or even in the visibility of corruption. The consensus came as a result of the emergence of a coalition of global players that see their interest in focusing on corruption. These global players are the US government, International Financial Institutions and big foreign investors. Each of them has their own reasons to focus on corruption. US government sees the anticorruption campaign as an instrument for promoting its trade interests. International Financial Institutions see in the anticorruption campaign an instrument for mobilizing support for their policies. Multinational companies see in the anticorruption campaign an opportunity to reduce the

---

9. Bibliography of the recent anticorruption studies can be found both on the websites of Transparency International and World Bank.

hidden protectionism in the emerging markets. It was this coalition of interests that made out of corruption a central policy issue. But it was the emergence of the Transparency International as a global anticorruption NGO, speaking with the voice of the "local" and the new date coming from the new anticorruption science that legitimized the new consensus that corruption is a global policy issue. The marginalization of the non-economic discourses on corruption became the major pre-condition for the emergence of the new anticorruption consensus.

The result is a new policy paradigm and a new rhetoric, which are beyond criticism. It is this lack of critical reflections on the global war on corruption that provoked my interest. The idea to study the making of the global anticorruption consensus came to me as a result of the striking observation that the anticorruption policies package promoted by the World Bank and IMF are basically the re-designed policies of the Washington consensus. The paradox is that local democracy activists who are otherwise restless to attack these policies became silent when these same policies came back to them dressed as anticorruption measures. Anticorruption rhetoric turned to be the major justification for the neoliberal policies in the field of economy and governing.

The consensus on corruption that is a consensus on the economic, social, and political costs of corruption was presented by IMF and World Bank as a consensus on causes for corruption and policies to curb it. What the global and local agreed upon was that endemic corruption hurts economic growth, increases social inequality and erodes democracy. At the same time there are two distinctively different anticorruption arguments.

The free market anticorruption argument is an argument against the corrupting effect of big government. "The growth of corruption—wrote Vito Tanzi —is the long term effect of the growth of the role of government in economy. I would hypothesize—he continues—that the impact that high taxes, a high level of spending, and new regulations have on the acts of corruption is not immediate, but rather a function of time" (Tanzi, 1998). Tanzi's hypothesis is at the heart of the Washington consensus on corruption. The rise of corruption is constructed as a long-term effect of the functioning of the interventionist state. Big government was singled out as the major source of corruption and the foundations for new global anticorruption policies were laid down. Economists started with the assumption that it is the big government that corrupts, so the next logical step was to suggest that the only successful anticorruption campaign is the withdrawal of government from economy.

The democracy anticorruption argument is an argument against the democracy deficit of the modern societies, but is also an argument against the excessive power of the market. It is not the big government that corrupts—it is the big money that corrupts. It is the illegal funding of the political parties, the criminal closeness between government and business that

causes corruption. The local civic activists traditionally view the war against corruption as the war between "the people" and "the interests." In the long
history of anticorruption rhetoric, it was much more
often this anti-market argument that has captured
public imagination.

The free market anticorruption argument is an argument that insists on deregulating the economic life
and withdrawal of the state. The democracy argument is the argument for effective state regulation
and effective limitation of the influence of money in
political process.

The two arguments are not necessarily contradic-
tory but they do not necessarily argue for the same
policy priorities. And they are not equally represented
in the global anticorruption campaign. Payments to
foreign officials, that distort the logic of competition,
are criminalized by the OECD convention, but payments to political parties and party officials that steal
the power of the voters are not excluded from OECD
convention criminalizing overseas bribery (Rose-Ackerman, 1999).

The free market anticorruption argument is an argument for less tax. The democracy argument is an
argument for more taxes, because rights have costs
(Holmes and Cass Sustain, 1999). You can easily rec-
oncile the free market and the democracy anticorruption arguments rhetorically, but you cannot at one
and the same time reduce and increase the taxes. The
perception that anticorruption consensus is beyond
the liberal–conservative divide is an illusionary one

In this respect the global anticorruption response prepared by the World Bank meets the logic of the free market argument but not always meets the logic of the democratic argument.

The question is why the "local" missed to see the asymmetry in the global response to corruption?

My answer is that this "blindness" has something to do with the very nature of corruption as political, economic, but also moral issue. As Anechiarico and Jacobs have powerfully argued in their book "The Pursuit of Absolute Integrity" the moral disgust with corruption is so high among the public and policy reformers that anticorruption policies are never object of cost-benefit studies. The moral costs of corruption are perceived as so high that any costs of the anticorruption policies are welcome. It is the "moral" character of the issue that keeps anticorruption campaigns beyond the usual procedures for policy accountability. The anticorruption discourse remains normative.

The new anticorruption knowledge additionally strengthens the normative character of the anticorruption policies. The new studies on corruption are mostly studies on the costs of corruption. They do not present strategy for anticorruption policies. The finding that corruption hurts economic growth does not give instructions of what to do about corruption. The studies on the political economy of the anticorruption reforms started to appear just in the last two years (Rose-Ackerman, 1999; World Bank, 2000). And some of their findings go against the priorities of the adopted anticorruption measures.

Designed as consensual and non-political, the global anticorruption policy package promoted by the World Bank resulted in re-cycling some of the most contested policies and aspects of the Washington consensus. The "local" was blind to notice the normative nature of the current anticorruption crusade because for them "corruption" was never normal policy issue. The "local" was hijacked by the rhetoric of anticorruption. In the ideas of democracy activists, anticorruption politics is by definition progressive and reformist.

Traveling back to my communist time memories, I have the depressive intuition that I have already experienced the mis-recognition of anticorruption campaign as genuine reform. It was in the distant 1980s when the Berlin wall was still there but there was an even higher wall between people and the communist government. The rhetoric of anticorruption was one of the few possible discourses of social criticism. Recognizing the crisis of confidence, communist authorities undertook massive anticorruption purges in an attempt to re-gain the confidence of the people (Leslie Holmes, 1993). Anticorruption rhetoric was reigning the cover pages of the government-controlled media. In the eyes of many of us it looked like reform. It turned out to be a failed attempt for counter-reform. It is this distant memory that made me cautious when anticorruption rhetoric started to dominate the policy debate. The global approach tends to de-politicize issues, turning them into problems for experts (read economists). And anticorruption politics tend to manufacture fake consensuses. But policies are not to be decided by experts only. And it is not enough to know that "God does not take bribes." At least this is how the democratic argument goes.

References

Anechiarico, Frank and James B. Jacobs. 1996. The Pursuit of Absolute Integrity: How Corruption Control Makes Government Ineffective. Chicago: University of Chicago Press.

Coulloudon, Virginie. 1997. "The Criminalization of Russian Political Elite." East European Constitutional Review 6:73–78.

De Sardan, Olivier J. P. 1999. "A Moral Economy of Corruption in Africa?" The Journal of Modern African Studies, 37, 1(1999), pp. 25–52.

Freeland, Chrystia. 2000. Sale of the Century. London: Little, Brown and Company.

Heidenheimer, Arnold, J. 1970. Political corruption: Readings in Comparative Analysis. New York: Holt, Rinehart and Winston, Inc.

Heywood, Paul (ed.), 1997. Political Corruption. Oxford: Blackwell Publishers.

Holmes, Leslie. 1993. The End of Communist Power: Anticorruption Campaigns and the Legitimation Crisis (Europe and the International Order). Oxford: Oxford University Press.

Holmes, Stephen & Cass R. Sunstein. 1999. The Cost of Corruption. New York, London: W.W Northon & Company.

Huntington, Samuel. 1968. Political Order in Changing Societies. New Haven, Connecticut: Yale University Press.

Kimberly Ann Elliot (ed.), 1997. Corruption and the Global Economy. Washington D.C.: Institute for International Economics.

Naim, Moises. 2000. "Washington Consensus or Washington Confusion." Foreign Policy, Spring: 87–101.

New Perspectives in Combating Corruption. 1998. A joint publication of the Transparency International and the Economic Development Institute of the World Bank.

Rose-Ackerman, Susan. 1999. Corruption and Government. Cambridge, UK: Cambridge University Press.

Tanzi, Vito. 1998. Corruption Around the World. Causes, Consequences, Scope, and Cures. IMF Staff Paper.

Visvanatan, S, Sethi, H (eds.), 1998. Foul Play. New Delhi: Banyan Books.

Wedel, Janine. 1998. Collision and Collusion: The Strange Case of Western Aid to Eastern Europe. New York: St. Martin's Press.

Williamson, John. 1990. "What Washington Means by Policy Reform." In John Williamson, (ed.), Latin American Adjustment: How Much Has Happened? Washington D.C.: Washington Institute for International Economics.

World Bank. 2000. Anticorruption in Transition. A Contribution to the Policy Debate. Washington D.C.: The World Bank.

Corruption, Anticorruption Sentiments and the Rule of Law

POST-COMMUNIST SOCIETIES ARE simply obsessed with corruption. Corruption is the most powerful policy narrative in the time of transition. It explains why industries that were once the jewels of the communist economies have bankrupted. Corruption explains why poor are poor and why rich are rich. Blaming corruption for the post-communist citizen is the only way to express his disappointment with the present political elites, to mourn the death of his 1989 expectations for better life, and to reject any responsibility for his present well being. Talking about corruption is the way post-communist public talks about politics, economy, about past and future.

Outsiders are even more obsessed with post-communist corruption. For many observers corruption explains why some transition countries succeed and others failed, why reforms are endangered and democracy is in risk, why people are unhappy and mafia is over-powerful. Rose, Mishler and Haerpfer argue that "corruption has replaced repression as the main threat to the rule of law" (Rose, Mishler, Haerpfer, 1997). Their multiple regression analysis suggests that the level of corruption is a more important determinant of attitudes towards "undemocratic alternatives" than the country's democratic tradition, its current level of freedom or its current economic performance. Corruption steals economic growth, erodes democracy, degrades society, and dooms the chances for the establishment of the rule of law society in Eastern Europe.

Corruption is the black myth of transition. It is the explanation of last resort for all failures and disappointments of the first post-communist decade. Rule of law is the white myth of transition. After some years of flirting with the ideas of democracy and market economy now rule of law is the magic phrase in Eastern Europe. It is rule of law and not democracy that brings foreign investors, it is rule of law that secures development and protects rights. It is the lack of rule of law that explains the spread of corruption and it is the march of rule of law that will guarantee success in the fight against corruption. What strikes in this new rule of law orthodoxy are the formalistic and anti-political overtones. Rule of law is not portrayed as a society in which rules of the game are respected and the rights of the citizens are protected but as a set of institutional devices and capacity building programs that should free people from the imperfection of democratic politics. And in this rule of law building exercise the special role is reserved for anticorruption campaigns. Anticorruption campaigns designed as achieving transparent institutions, raising public awareness and building institutional capacities are viewed by the World Bank and other external policy makers as the critical strategy for promoting the rule of law state. But are the anticorruption campaigns the shortest cut to the rule of law culture and are we aware of the hidden risks of such campaign? The major argument of this article is that the current policy thinking misunderstands the effects of anticorruption campaigns and by this blurs the prospects for the establishment of rule of law culture in Eastern Europe. The central reason for this misunderstanding is the misreading of the nature of the public's anticorruption sentiments.

It is the analysis of the moral economy of the anticorruption sentiments in the period of transition and a close reading of the attempts to create socialist legal state in the early 1980s that can enlighten us on the dark side of the current obsession with fighting corruption.

The present paper is not a study of corruption, neither a study of a rule of law politics, it is an interpretation of the anxieties of transition. It is a reflection on the popular discourse on corruption and its role in making post-communist society. Anticorruption discourse is not simply a discourse on the real or alleged acts of bribery or other forms of misusing public office for private gains. It can not be reduced to the unarticulated public disappointment with the status quo. It is a discourse expressing the painful process of social stratification in the transition societies. It is a discourse on social equality and fairness. It is a set of discourses, conflicting with each other and re-constituting the meaning of post-communist corruption.

The anticorruption pronouncements of the international financial institutions have almost nothing in common with the anticorruption outcries hosted in the tabloid media, heard on the streets or captured in the focus groups. What is corruption, who corrupts whom, what are the reasons for the rise of corruption and what should be done to curb it are among the questions that will receive different answers depending on whom you ask in post-communist society.

"It would be impossible for an historian to write a history of political corruption in the United States" noted Walter Lippmann in 1930. "What we could write is the history of the exposure of corruption." It would be also impossible for a historian to write a history of political corruption in post-communist Eastern Europe. What we could write is the history of policy responses to corruption and what we can speculate on is the long term effects of these responses.

The Corruption Paradox

It was a commonplace among the ordinary citizens of the Soviet block to view corruption and privileges as the most disgusting features of "real socialism." Privileges were for the nomenclature, corruption was for the people. People complained about it, lived with it and protested against it. In academic writing communism was also described as highly corrupted. Dependence on bribes and contacts was notorious. Towards the end of the communist regime, a majority of respondents in DiFranceisco and Gitelman's survey of Soviet émigrés suggested that bribery or connections could be used to change an unwelcome work assignment or to get a dull child into a good university department (Miller, Grodeland, Koshechkina, 2001).

A decade ago both public and scholars would have been shocked to learn that one day post-communism would be seen as more corrupt than communism. It is this transformation of the "unexpected" into "unproblematic" in the perception of corruption that I refer to as "corruption paradox."

The Non-Banality of Post-Communist Corruption

What is common between the successful Polish transition, semi-successful Bulgarian transition and unsuccessful Russian transition? Not much, except that the majority of Poles, Bulgarians and Russians are convinced that in their country there is more corruption today than in the days of communism.

The figures are striking because Polish, Bulgarian and Russian public opinions sharply differ in the way they judge the success and the direction of the economic and political changes, the desirability of changes, and also their personal benefits and loses in the period of transition. The result is striking also because in the Corruption Perception Index of TI for 1999 Poland ranks 44 on the level of corruption. Bulgaria ranks 66 and Russia 82 and because corruption is figured out as a major social problem in Bulgaria and Poland, but not in Russia (Sajó, 1998).

The claim that post-communism is more corrupt than communism can not be explained simply with the failure of market reforms. The success or failure of reforms can be a working explanatory model when we compare the scale of corruption in different countries, but it is a weak explanation when we compare "now" and "then." Culture, religion, the length of the communist rule are also non-explanations. Poland is a catholic society, Bulgaria and Russia are Orthodox countries. Russia has lived much longer under communism than Bulgaria and Poland. Countries differ significantly in their size and ethnic homogeneity, two other factors that affect the spread of corruption. They differ in GDP, attractiveness to foreign investment, availability of natural resources and level of economic optimism with respect to the future. The finding that Bulgarians, Poles and Russian share the common view that post-communism is more corrupt than communism is an unexpected finding, a nontrivial one. It is worth closer exploration.

Corruption can not be studied directly. The indirect studies of corruption are also problematic. What do we claim when we assert that certain regime or certain period is more corrupt than the other? Do we claim that during this period the number of corrupt transactions has increased? Do we claim that the number of people involved in corrupt transactions has increased? Do we claim that corruption has reached the highest places of power? Do we claim that the social costs of corruption have increased? Do we claim that society as a whole is more tolerant to corruption, or do we claim all these together?

How can we know what exactly the respondent wants to tell us when judging that post-communism is more corrupt than communism? Does he refer to the cost of corruption, to the ugliness of the grand political corruption or to pervasive bureaucratic corruption? Is his judgment based on his personal experience with petty corruption or is his claim based on the media stories about the scale of political corruption? It is also well known that the popularity of corruption practices increase the levels of their acceptability. If almost everybody is a practicing corrupter or corrupee, then corruption is a rule and not a deviation from the rule. Does it mean that communism looks less corrupt because everybody was part of corruption games?

And finally, is post-communism really more corrupt than communism? The empirical data is controversial and incomplete to sustain such a claim. In most of the communist countries corruption was a topic taboo, so the reliable data on perceptions of corruption or facts based reports on the spread of corruption acts are not available. The court and the police records can not be a source of valid information. Most of them are silent with respect to corruption when it comes to the high-ranking communist officials. Communism was a political system based on virtue, so the regime was unwilling to demonstrate the human vulnerability of its outstanding members.

And what kind of definition will be adopted for the purpose of comparison? Should we consider only the corrupt acts that are criminalized in the given period? Should we count only acts that are perceived as corrupt by public opinion, what Heidenheimer called "white corruption" (Heidenheimer, 1989), or should we adopt a more general public interest definition that will define as corruption all those acts that are viewed as corruption today? In interpreting corruption we should face all these and many other constrains.

The Debate

In the current debate various approaches compete in explaining and constructing corruption phenomenon. They legislate how to think about corruption, what to think about corruption and how to act against corruption. The dominant anticorruption discourse of IMF and World Bank is institutional in its nature. For it the claim that one political regime is more corrupt than other is not an empirical claim. It is a normative claim. The prevailing institutional discourse measures corruption through the corruption incentives created by various institutional environments. In the context of this approach regime A is more corrupt than regime B if the discretionary power of public officials and the level of state intervention is higher in regime A in comparison with regime B.

The dissident or perceptionalist view on the rise of corruption is limited in its influence and is perceived by many as the last incarnation of the "apologists" of corruption. This discourse is not interested in the incentives for corruption behavior that are made available by different political regimes. It starts with the assumption that there is no necessary link between the perception of the public that corruption is pervasive and the actual level of corruption. In the context of this school of thought corruption perception is a product of a given media reality (in the broader sense) and not of any significant changes in the actual spread of corruption. Perception change in Germany in the wake of the "Kohl affair" is a powerful illustration of the fact that it is the corruption which we know about and not the actual level of corruption that governs public sentiments. Germany after the breaking out of the Kohl scandal is not more corrupt than Germany in the day before the story was revealed, but the perception of the cleanness of the Berlin Republic has declined dramatically both inside and outside the country. The perceptionalist argument distrusts the consensus that corruption is in the rise. In their seminal study of street level corruption in four East European countries Muller, Grodeland and Koshechkina documented that citizens' actual experience of dealing with street-level corruption is far less negative than their perceptions (Miller et al., 2001).

My interpretation of the boom of corruption perceptions in Eastern Europe does not side either with the institutionalists or with perceptionalists. It agrees that the link between corruption perceptions and the actual levels of corruption is highly problematic: but it suggests that when the public compares corruption "now" and "then" it does not simply "count" corrupt acts neither does it "count" corruption related media materials. The judgment on the rise or decline of corruption is mediated by reflections on its social functions. Interpreting opinion's claim that post-communism is more corrupt than communism needs to bring in the broader context of actors' experience of social change. Numbers and correlations are not enough for reading public mind. It is in the course of the endless talks about corruption, the corrupted and the government's failure to resist corruption that post-communist citizens negotiate their attitude to the phenomenon. And in the course of these invisible negotiations the consensus that post-communism is more corrupt than communism is being reached.

When Less State Does Not Mean Less Corruption

In arguing that the actual corruption in Eastern Europe has increased, political scientists and economists point to several recent developments. Internalization of trade and finance and the end of grand ideological divide counts for external reasons for "corruption eruption." But there are several "transition" arguments for the rise of corruption.

The communist legacy and particularly the legacy of the interventionist state is singled out as the critical domestic pre-condition for the rise of corruption. Post-communist regimes as a rule have inherited a lot of license permission and discretionary power for state officials. The existence of these discretionary regimes is at the core of the institutional explanation of corruption eruption (Tanzi, 1998).

The crisis of legitimacy and the low trust in the public institutions is the other part of the explanation. The existence of corruption incentives can not be directly translated into claims for more corruption. Values do matter. The Nordic countries that are known for the significant presence of the state in the economy are among the most corruption-free countries in the world. Corruption incentives increase the actual level of corruption only when they are in partnership with public tolerance to corruption and absence of professional bureaucracy and rule of law. Social norms are the independent variable in corruption equation that constrains the ambitions of institutional reductionism.

But not only big government but also weak states contribute to the pervasive corruption in Eastern Europe. A weak state lacks the capacity to enforce rules and dramatically diminishes the risks connected with corrupt behavior. Weak state is at the heart of the argument developed by Shliefer and Vishny (Shliefer and Vishny, 1993). In their article "Corruption" they suggest that post-communist corruption is more inefficient than the communist one and as a result, it is more costly. Communist corruption was a centralized one. It was enough to bribe the boss in order to set the chain in action. The model of post-communist corruption is the model of the independent monopolists. In order to make the transaction happen the corrupter should bribe almost everybody in the chain.

Another argument explaining the rise of corruption in the transition period is the argument of the Hungarian constitutionalist András Sajó (Sajó, 1998). He suggests that post-communist corruption is clientelistic in its nature and is closely connected with the forming of the political parties and re-distribution of state assets. Corruption is the hidden tax that society pays for the functioning of the multi-party system. Mis-recognition of clientelism for corruption and Western pressure for transparency is the reasons for over-dramatization of the East European corruption problem.

But it is the large-scale privatization that dominates popular explanations for the rise of corruption in the time of transition. Theoretically, and in a long run, privatization is advertised as a corruption reducing policy (Kaufman, 1997). But practically and in a short run privatization increases the level of corruption. The incentives for quick enrichment are so high that corrupt behavior is unavoidable. Polish Minister of Privatization Janusz Lewandowski gave one of the best descriptions of the internal controversy of the process. "Privatization—wrote Lewandowski—is when someone who does not know who the real owner is and does not know what it is really worth sells something to someone who does not have any money" (Dunn, 1999). Lewandowski's definition touches the three troubles with the post-communist privatization. The first is the pricing of the ex-socialist property. The prices of the socialist enterprises differ dramatically in the eyes of the market and in the eyes of society. The complaint that the state is selling "cheap" is the most popular complaint in the time of transition. In her study of workers' perception of privatization in one Polish food producing factory Elizabeth Dunn underlines that "the idea of the 'bribe' here is the difference between two distinct measures of value: the supposedly 'objective' measure set by Western accounting or by the market, and Alima workers' subjective opinion of the value of their lives and work under socialism, which were crystallized in the firm" (Dunn, 1999).

The second trouble is the buyers. Domestic buyers for the big and even middle-sized enterprises did not exist in Eastern Europe. Real socialism was not the society of equal prosperity but in the beginning of transition many people still believed that it was the society of equal poverty. It was in the initial years of transition that some got access to credit and became buyers and others remained on the side of the selling state. The past of the new owners intrigued public imagination much more than the future of the privatized enterprises. And the third trouble with privatization is that the very process of privatization was conceived by many as a corruption per se. The absence of effective control on the black and gray privatization practices acted as a catalyst in rising anticorruption and anti-elite sentiments. In a 12-month period one Czech study identified 33 cases of personal gain in the area of privatization totaling 25 billion Czech crowns but it resulted in only two prosecutions (Miller et al., 2001).

Bulgarian economist Rumen Avramov defined "privatization of the profits and nationalization of losses" as the major formula for creating the private sector in post-communist Eastern Europe (Avramov, 2001).

The virtual school in explaining "corruption eruption" suggests different readings of the post-communist obsession with corruption. A number of studies stress the fact that there is low correlation between respondents' personal experience with corruption and their judgment on the level of corruption in the country (Miller et al., 2001). The regular newspaper readers in Bulgaria estimate the country as more corrupt than those who do not regularly read newspapers. Miller, Grodeland and Koshechkina documented that contrary to the proverb, familiarity bred trust rather than contempt. People tend to view as less corrupt those institutions that they know personally and as more corrupt institutions that are far away from their daily experience. As a result the Parliament as a rule is viewed as more corrupt than police. In a paradoxical way free media is an instrument for controlling and reducing corruption but at the same time it increases corruption perceptions in the society.

Perceptionalist argument suggests that the boom in corruption perceptions is a result of the media's obsession with corruption and the role of corruption accusations in post-communist politics. Corruption stories sell well. The public loves reading stories of degradation. But commercial explanation is not sufficient. In the time of transition when grand ideological divide is already in history and when policy differences between main political parties are negligible corruption accusations are the major weapons of the opposition. To accuse government of being corrupt saves the need to offer alternative to its policies. There is in Eastern Europe today a distinct prejudice in favor of those who make the accusations. The number of court verdicts on corruption charges is ridiculously small all over the region. The non-functioning legal system gives the media the role of both prosecutor and a judge. In the post-communist world anticorruption rhetoric is the favorite weapon for anybody seeking power.

In the context of the institutional paradigm transition period creates high incentives for corrupt behavior and the weak post-communist state constantly fails to respond efficiently. The virtual argument reduces the rise of corruption perception to the information asymmetry. Both arguments are vulnerable in their explanations why post-communist public opinion is convinced that "today" is more corrupt than "yesterday."

Institutional arguments underestimate the role of social and cultural norms in restraining corruption. The virtual argument overestimates the lack of genuine information in the time of late communism. The fact that official channels of information were blocked does not mean that people were ignorant about the spread of corruption in their society. The unofficial discourse has recorded many corruption stories. So, we need to include the perspective of the participant in order to offer more convincing interpretation to the corruption paradox. The real question is not whether post-communism is more corrupt than communism, the real question is why public opinion judges post-communism to be more corrupt than communism.

The Moral Economy of Corruption—
"Now" and "Then"

The introduction of the actors' perspective in interpreting public opinion's view on corruption is the only alternative to institutional and virtual explanations. But the introduction of the actors' perspective is an uneasy task. The data of anthropological studies and focus groups is contextual and heterogenious and the risks for misinterpretations are grave. Respondents that claim that post-communism is more corrupt than communism do not share common view on what should be and should not be defined as corruption. They come from various social backgrounds and their tolerance with respect to corruption varies. Reconstructing individual motivations for blaming post-communism for being more corrupt than communism is mission impossible.

The general hypothesis in my essay is that the claim expressed by the respondents that post-communism is more corrupt than communism is not a factual claim. It is a value statement that includes in itself reflection on the social function of corruption.

Respondents do not simply "register" corruption, they judge the result of its work. The key factor explaining the new corruption sensitivity is that one specific type of corruption has been replaced by a radically different form of corruption. Blat was replaced by bribery.

Interpretation of the "corruption paradox" necessarily pre-supposes comparison of respondents' perception of "blat" and "bribe" as the dominant forms of corruption respectively in the communist and post-communist periods.

"Do Me A Favor Society" versus "Give Me A Bribe Society"

The mysterious and at the same time prosaic practices that Russians called "blat," Bulgarians called "connections" and Poles called "zalatwic sprawy" are known to be the secret key for understanding the communist society. Society in which, according to Guardian reporter Martin Walker "nothing is legal but everything is possible" (Ledeneva, 1998).

In her enlightening book "Russia's Economy of Favors" Alena Ledeneva defines "blat" as "the use of personal networks and informal contacts to obtain goods and services in short supply and to find a way around formal procedures" (Ledeneva, 1998). All authors agree that blat is a typically Soviet (communist) phenomenon. Blat shares many similarities to premodern practices of gift giving and many theorists (like most of the citizens) are unenthusiastic to classify blat as corruption. "Adultery is not a crime and blat is not a corruption" is the shared opinion among most of the participants in focus groups. But in its essence blat is a classical form of misuse of public position for private or group gains. Blat works to the extent to which certain public officials betray their duties in order to favor their friends or friends of their friends.

In her remarkable book Ledeneva presents a complex analysis of the phenomenon and its role for the survival and erosion of the Soviet system. In the context of my interest in revealing the moral economy of anticorruption sentiments in Eastern Europe several characteristics of blat are of critical importance. Blat was well-spread phenomenon all over the Soviet block. Living out of blat was a form of asocial behavior. Blat was an exchange of favors. Even when some gifts and money were involved in the blat relations it was the exchange of favors and not the bribe that were the driving force of the relations. In the words of Ledeneva "blat is distinctive form of non-monetary exchange, a kind of barter based on personal relations" (Ledeneva, 1998). Blat was totally conditioned on the economy of shortages. It was "survival kit reducing uncertainty in conditions of shortage, exigency and perpetual emergency, in which formal criteria and formal rights are insufficient to operate" (Ledeneva, 1998). Blat was condemned in the official discourse but it is not criminalized (with the exception of extreme cases). Blat relations were not simple barter, they were not necessary dyadic. Blat transactions could be circular: A provides a favor to B, B to C, C to D, and D to A, and the last chain might not have taken place. Blat exchange is mediated and covered by the rhetoric of friendship. In contrast, the relationship between corrupter and corrupee is centered on bribe.

In the days of communism blat coexisted with bribe and other classical forms of corruption. But blat was the most popular type of surviving strategy. Blat was the paradigmatic form of corruption. Communism was totalitarianism moderated by the spread of blat and petty bribery. When respondents reflect on their communist experience blat comes as the form of corruption they associate with the old regime. Participants in different focus groups insist that the practice of "connections" was widely spread in the old days, but the acts of "real corruption" were much more limited than now.

In her book Ledeneva even argues that blat should not be classified as corruption. Such a view can be found also when people tell their own blat experience. Personal friendship and readiness to help colored participants' blat memories. Ledeneva's argument is valuable in distinguishing blat from other forms of informal transactions. But it is also true that blat was perceived as corruption and that blat involves abuse of public office for private gains. Corruption was simply other people's blat. In the popular discourse "other people's blat" was commented and viewed as a corruption. When mother was telling the story why her kid failed to enter university, when a customer complained about not "obtaining" valuable goods privileges and "connections" were the explanations and they were judged as corruption.

The anticorruption campaigns that were common feature of the late days of the communist regimes best illustrate the fact that blat was perceived as a specific form of corruption and as a practice which erodes public good. The citizen of communist society was aware of the social price of blat but he was also aware of the lack of any other realistic alternative for surviving.

The disappearance of blat is the key development for understanding the post-communist corruption reality. "Market conditions have changed personal relations and ruined many friendships—stated one of Russians interviewed by Ledeneva—there is no room for blat as it used to be. It looks like blat won't be the same and the very word is going into oblivion." Results of the opinion polls show that blat is loosing its significance (Ledeneva, 1998; Miller et al., 2001). The end of the economy of shortage and the rise of the "real money" changed the rules of the game. The major process observed in all transition countries is the monetarization of the blat relations and replacement of blat by bribe. The economy of favors was replaced by the economy of paid services. The transition re-discovered the unrestricted power of money. So, it is not surprising that former communist societies reacted to the monetarization of blat in the same way the pre-modern societies reacted in their earlier encounters with modernity (Avramov, 2001).

In my interpretation the perception inside the transition societies that post-communism is more corrupt than communism is linked to the fact that bribes replaced blat as the dominant form of corruption. Blat networks are re-organized on market principles. Blat networks are transformed into classical corruption networks involved in the redistribution of the state assets while other blat networks simply disappeared. Personal interests have become business interests. In the view of one of the participants in Ledeneva's survey "finance, licenses, privileged loans, access to business information are the shortages of today" (Ledeneva, 1998).

The critical question is what makes blat and bribe so different in the perception of the post-communist public. Umit Berkman has stressed that corruption behavior is conditioned by the nature of the corrupt act (Miller et al., 2001).

The non-monetary character of blat is critical in understanding its social acceptability. Citizens are easier offering presents than money. And officials are more easily asking for favors than for money (Miller et al., 2001).

But the social acceptability of blat can not be reduced to its non-monetary character. In the last years of socialism bribe money was making its carrier in the blat relations. It is the latent functions of blat and bribes in respectively the communist and the post-communist system that explain the distinction.

Blat is a socially acceptable form of corruption not simply because it is non-monetary form of corruption but because it increases the social equality in the communist society. It "allows" participants in blat transactions to mis-recognize their activities as "help" and to cover it in the rhetoric of friendship.

In most of the studies blat is analyzed as an exchange of services and information. Blat was the only channel for the unprivileged to obtain deficit goods. It was viewed as a form of protest against the communist regime. But what is even more important is that blat was also an exchange of social statuses. In the economy of deficit the power status of the person was defined on one side by his position on the power vertical (being in or out the nomenclature) but on the other side by the access to deficit goods or information. Blat destroyed the dependence of consumption on the place in hierarchy. On the queue for popular but deficit book, it is not the professor, or the senior official but the friend of the bookseller who usually won the bid.

In its radical form blat has replaced the relations between public roles with relations between people.

This redistribution of power sustained and subverted the system in the same time. It made life bearable but it undermined the power relations. Loyalty to one's blat network was higher than loyalty to the state. Using the present jargon blat empowered the powerless.

In the discourse of the majority of the people "connections" were unfair but they were the only way to "humanize" the bureaucratic nature of the regime. The word "bureaucracy" had a connotation more negative than connections. The discourse on communist time corruption was a discourse of inclusion.

The social functions of bribe in the post-communist reality are contrary to the functions of blat. Bribe caused the inflation of the social capital defined as blat. Monetarization of social relation led to the inflation of the social investments that ordinary citizen has put in their blat networks. Only blat networks of the powerful survived in the new conditions. The market deprived the bookseller from his power. The end of the shortage economy inflated bookseller's shares in the blat cooperative. Now he has nothing to offer except his friendship. It is also much costly to sustain previous blat networks. Blat was conditioned not only on the economy of shortages but also on the low costs of communications, coffee and the unrestricted availability of free time. Now it is not possible any more to spend long hours on telephone talking about nothing and to leave the office any time your friend wants to see you.

The transition from blat to bribery was painful for

post-communist societies. Bribery can not be covered under the rhetoric of friendship and this makes people feel morally uncomfortable. Bribe contributes to the social stratification making it easier for the rich to obtain what they want. "Corruption causes a distinction; in reality there should exist no difference" stated a participant in a focus group discussion in Sofia. Inequalities of wealth provide the means to pay bribes, while inequalities of power provide the means to extort them (Miller et al., 2001).

Why public opinion in Eastern Europe perceives post-communism as more corrupt than communism? This essay argues for a complex answer. Public judges about corruption not by counting corruption acts or corruption related media stories. Judgment on corruption is mediated by the social functions of corruption in society. The dramatic change of corruption perception in Eastern Europe in the last decade can not be explained simply with the actual rise of corruption or the boom of media's interest in corruption. Anticorruption sentiments in Eastern Europe were provoked by the fact that bribe has replaced blat as a paradigmatic form of corruption. Blat is viewed by the public as a socially more acceptable form of corruption. It was the non-monetary character of blat and its role for re-distributing goods and power that made it look more legitimate in the eyes of the public opinion. Bribery is less acceptable not only because it is more ugly (aesthetically), or because it is more risky (in legal terms). Bribery is less acceptable because it is a mechanism for producing social inequality. World Bank report states that "inequality within the transition countries has increased in alarming pace. In some countries of the region inequality has now reached levels on par with the most unequal Latin American countries" (World Bank, 2000).

The popular anticorruption discourse is not a discourse on transparency or good government, it is a discourse on the rise of inequality. This is the reason why anticorruption discourse is the most popular discourse to criticize market and democracy in a society in which market and democracy do not have an alternative.

The Rule of Law Paradox

In the early 1980s three strange "criminals" shared a cell in Lefortovo prison in Moscow. They perfectly well symbolized the three most dangerous enemies of the communist system. Lev Timofeev was dissident and economist writing on corruption as institutional problem in communist society. Vahab Usmanov was a top Soviet official, former minister of cotton in Uzbekistan, who in 1986 was executed for corruption and abuse of power. The third inhabitant of the cell was of less importance. He was a former University professor who was arrested for currency speculations and money extraction from his foreign students (Timofeev, 2000). All three stayed in prison at the time when Soviet authorities inspired by Andropov tried to use anticorruption campaigns and anticorruption rhetoric as an instrument for replacing the ideological legitimization of the regime with a rational-legal legitimization. The ultimate goal was the creation of a socialist legal state (Leslie Holmes). All three were skeptical about the chances of the undertaking. The ex-minister was struggling to understand why somebody should be put in prison for doing what all senior party officials usually do. It was true that Usmanov was taking bribes and he did not deny it, but was it possible not to take bribes when you should give bribes. The success or failures of Uzbek cotton production depended on the success of the bribe-mediated bargains in the Plan Committee and other federal institutions. For Usmanov anticorruption campaign was a form of the leadership war. Timofeev was also unable to grasp the logic of the undertaking. For him it was a mystery how Soviet leadership was planning to fight corruption when the very existence of the Soviet system depended on the existence of the black markets of goods and power. The third prisoner did not have specific argument for mistrusting the anticorruption campaign but he has a general argument, he mistrusted anything that the government did.

The prisoners were right in their skepticism. Andropov initiated anticorruption campaign and the officially tolerated anticorruption rhetoric did not increase the trust in the government on the opposite they contributed to the de-legitimization and the collapse of the communist system.

In my view there is also room for skepticism that anticorruption campaigns are the shortest path to rule of law culture in Eastern Europe.

An unavoidable trait of the anticorruption campaign is the constantly expanding definition of corruption. If in the beginning of the campaign the suspicion is that the corruption is almost everywhere, already in the middle of the campaign the suspicion is that corruption is almost everything. The final stage is the conviction that almost everybody is corrupt. The fear of corruption accusation paralyses the energy of the government officials and the major objective of the policy makers is to opt for solutions that look clean nevertheless of what other disadvantages they can have. Making "transparency" the ultimate policy incentive explains why Bulgarian government in the last two years became in favor of the auction type of privatization. The criticism that such type of privatization is not the best option for attracting strategic investors and preventing criminal money to enter the process have been ignored. For the government it was more important to prove cleanness than to go for better economic option.

The second disadvantage of the anticorruption campaigns is that focusing on corruption they contribute to the blurring of the lines between different political options. Corruption-centered politics in a way is the end of politics. It moralizes the policy choices to the extent that politics is reduced to the choice between corrupt government and clean opposition. Corruption-centered politics is one of the explanations for the transformation of East European democracy into protest vote democracies.

The third disadvantage of the anticorruption campaigning that results in increasing de-legitimization of the political elite and public administration is that a number of young and talented people who in different environments would choose politics or public administration as their vocation under present conditions prefer to stay away from the realm of the corrupted. The claim that politicians are corrupt by definition is supported by the majority of respondents in the public opinion polls in countries like Bulgaria, Romania and Macedonia.

Since corruption is a crime very difficult to prove, the current focus on corruption leads to the re-distribution of powers, i.e., to increase the powers of investigating agencies. Loyal to the principles of the rule of law, courts face difficulty imposing corruption sentences. There is a huge difference between the politicians accused in the media and the politicians sentenced in the court. The pressure for spectacular verdicts in the war against corruption comes into conflict with the fact that corruption is one of the most difficult crimes to prove in court. In Bulgaria practically all ministers that have been in office for the last ten years are investigated or have been investigated by prosecution for corruption-related allegation, but there is no single minister in prison. The result is growing mistrust in the judicial system and growing accusations that the judicial system is totally corrupt.

Contrary to the expectations and intentions of the architects of the post-communist anticorruption campaigns, crusade against corruption can be as harmful to the emergence of rule of law culture in Eastern Europe as is the corruption itself. The anticorruption rhetoric creates expectations that can not be met by the results of the anticorruption policies and the major reason for the vicious circle that emerges is the nature of the anticorruption sentiments in the period of transition. Anticorruption sentiments are driven not by the actual level of corruption but by the general disappointment with the changes and the rising social inequality. It is this weak correlation between the world of corruption and the world of anticorruption sentiments that questions the usefulness of the anticorruption campaigns. What post-communist societies need are policies that reduce corruption but not a rhetoric that leads to corruption-centered politics.

References

Avramov, Rumen. 2001. Stopanskia XX vek na Bulgaria. Sofia: Centre for Liberal Strategies.

Coulloudon, Virginie. 1997. "The Criminalization of Russia's Political Elite." East European Constitutional Review 6:73–78.

De Sardan, Olivier J. P. 1999. "A Moral Economy of Corruption in Africa?" The Journal of Modern African Studies, 37, 1(1999), 25–52.

Dunn, Elizabeth. 1999. "Audit, Corruption, and the Problem of Personhood: Scenes From Postsocialist Poland." Lecture in the Wissenchaftskolleg, Berlin.

"European Bank for Reconstruction and Development. 2000." Transition Report 2000: Employment, Skills and Transition. London: EBRD.

Grødeland, Åse B., Tatyana Y. Koshechkina, William L. Miller. 1998. "'Foolish to Give and Yet More Foolish Not to Take'—In-depth Interviews with Post-Communist Citizens on Their Everyday Use of Bribes and Contacts." Europe-Asia Studies 50:651–677.

Hellman, Joel S., Geraint Jones, Daniel Kaufmann. 2000. "Seize the State, Seize the Day": State Capture, Corruption, and Influence in Transition. Policy research Working Paper 2444, Washington DC: World Bank.

Holmes, Leslie. 1993. The End of Communist Power: Anti-corruption Campaigns and Legitimation Crisis. Cambridge, UK: Policy Press.

Ledeneva, Alena V. 1998. Russia's Economy of Favors: Blat, Networking and Informal Exchanges. Cambridge, UK: Cambridge University Press.

Meny, Yves. 2000. "Fin de siecle Corruption: Change, Crisis and Shifting Values." In Williams, R (ed.) Explaining Corruption. Cheltenham, UK: Edward Elgar Publishing Limited.

Miller, William L., Åse B. Grødeland, and Tatyana Y. Koshechkina. 1997. "How Citizens Cope with Postcommunist Official: Evidence from Focus Group Discussions in Ukraine and the Czech Republic." Political Studies 45:597–625.

Miller, William L., Åse B. Grødeland, and Tatyana Y. Koshechkina. 1998a. "Are People Victims or Accomplices? The Use of Presents and Bribes to Influence Officials in Eastern Europe." Crime, Law, and Social Change 29:273–310.

Miller, William L., Åse B. Grødeland, and Tatyana Y. Koshechkina. 1999a. "Confessions: A Model of Officials' Perspectives on Accepting Gifts from Clients in Post-Communist Europe." Paper presented at the Coalition 2000 Conference in Varna, 19–20 June.

Miller, William L., Åse B. Grødeland, and Tatyana Y. Koshechkina. 1999b. "A Focus Group Study of Bribery and Other Ways of Coping with Officialdom in Postcommunist Eastern Europe." Paper presented at the Coalition 2000 Conference in Varna, 19–20 June.

Miller, William L., Åse B. Grødeland, and Tatyana Y. Koshechkina. 2001. A Culture of Corruption: Coping with Government in Post-Communist Europe. Budapest, New York: Central European University Press.

Mishler, William, and Richard Rose. 1997. "Trust, Distrust, and Skepticism: Popular Evaluation of Civil and Political Institutions in Post-Communist Societies." Journal of Politics 59(2):418–51.

Mishler, William, and Richard Rose. 1998. Trust in Untrustworthy Institutions: Culture and Institutional Performance in Post-Communist Societies. Studies in Public Policy Number 310, Centre for the Study of Public Policy, University of Strathcylde, Glasgow, Scotland.

Philp, Mark. 2000. "Defining Political Corruption." In Williams, R. (ed.) Explaining Corruption. Cheltenham, UK: Edward Elgar Publishing Limited.

Rose, Richard. 1999b. New Russia Barometer: Trends Since 1992. Studies in Public Policy 320, Centre for the Study of Public Policy, University of Strathclyde, Glasgow.

Rose, Richard, and Christian Haerpfer. 1998a. New Democracies Barometer V: A 12-Nation Survey. Studies in Pubic Policy 306, Centre for the Study of Public Policy, University of Strathclyde, Glasgow.

Rose, Richard, and Christian Haerpfer. 1998b. Trends in Democracies and Markets: New Democracies Barometer 1991–1998. Studies in Pubic Policy 308, Centre for the Study of Public Policy, University of Strathclyde, Glasgow.

Rose, Richard, William Mishler, and Christian Haerpfer. 1997. Getting Real: Social Capital in Post-Communist Societies. Studies in Pubic Policy 278, Centre for the Study of Public Policy, University of Strathclyde, Glasgow.

Rose-Ackerman, Susan. 1994. "Reducing Bribery in the Public Sector." In Duc V. Trang, (ed.), Corruption and Democracy. Budapest: Institute for Constitutional and Legislative Policy, 21–28.

Rose-Ackerman, Susan. 1999. Corruption and Government: Causes, Consequences and Reform. Cambridge UK: Cambridge University Press.

Sajó, András. 1998. "Corruption, Clientelism and the Future of Constitutional State in Eastern Europe." East European Constitutional Review vol. 7, no. 2.

Shleifer, Andre, and Robert Vishny. 1993. "Corruption." Quarterly Journal of Economics 108:599–617.

Sztompka, Piotr. 1999. Trust: A Sociological Theory. Cambridge UK: Cambridge University Press.

Timofeev, Lev. 2000. Institutcionalnata Korupcia. Moscow: Moscow State University Press.

World Bank. 2000. Anticorruption in Transition: A Contribution to the Policy Debate. Washington D.C.: The World Bank.

The Missing Incentive:
Corruption, Anticorruption,
and Reelection

ANTICORRUPTION CAMPAIGNS in post-communist democracies are running out of steam. There is a silent consensus that the war on corruption has failed to obtain the expected results. "Though still in the early stages of development, the experience of anti-corruption programs to date has produced mixed results. ... Ambitious anticorruption campaigns in several countries have floundered at the implementation stage. Key structural reforms have been blocked by powerful vested interests. In some cases, politicians have hijacked the anticorruption agenda and used it to attack their rivals," stated a World Bank report (World Bank, 2000: 15). "The political economy of anticorruption initiatives has proven complex and difficult" (p. 31). The conclusion reached is that "a serious anticorruption program cannot be imposed from the outside, but requires committed leadership from within, ideally from the highest levels of the state. While pressure for reform can come from below, any effective program must be supported from the top" (p. 30).

Why anticorruption programs are not getting support from "the top" is the central question of this paper. It is not a study of anticorruption policies. It is a study of incentives. The "highest levels of the state" do not support anticorruption efforts (1) because they have incentives to be involved in corruption, or (2) because they do not have incentives to initiate anti-corruption campaigns even when they do not have incentives to be involved in corruption. These two hypotheses are distinctively different. What interests us is the second hypothesis. We adopt the perspective of the government and not of the individual politician as the focus of research. We define the government as a vote maximizer. In the framework of our study the self-interest of the government is to be reelected.

Why post-communist governments have incentives to be involved in corruption is a problem that was the subject of several studies (see, for example, della Porta and Vannucci, 1999; Sajó, 2002). In our paper we only refer to these studies. "Do democratic governments in post-communist Eastern Europe have incentives to launch anticorruption campaigns?" is the question that really interested us.

The assumption behind the present anticorruption policies endorsed by the World Bank is that success-ful anticorruption campaigns increase the chances of democratic governments to be reelected. When it "sells" its anticorruption policy World Bank relies on the self-interest of the governments and not on their high morality. That is why the current failure of the anticorruption programs has contributed to the lack of political will and to the institutional weakness of the governments in transition countries. The possibility that uncorrupt governments do not have incentives to launch anticorruption campaigns was never discussed.

The present paper tests that silent assumption. The result was unexpected: it turned out that translating successful anticorruption policies into electoral advantage is the principal difficulty. The launching of anticorruption campaigns does not improve the re-election chances of the government, regardless of the fact that society is in favor of anticorruption politics and that the government sincerely implements anticorruption policies.

We do not in this paper elaborate on the different definitions of corruption.[1] We accept that corruption is an abuse of public office for private gains (Heidenheimer, 1999; Rose-Ackerman, 1999). We view it as a result of "a network of illegal exchanges" (della Porta and Vannucci, 1999: 20–21). And to the extent to which political corruption is at the center of our study we follow Claus Offe who defines political corruption as the "selling and buying of public decisions" (Offe, 2002).

We study corruption and anticorruption primarily as political/electoral resources. We do not focus on the individual corrupt act. We consider the personal enrichment of corrupt politicians as a side effect of the decision of political parties to adopt corruption as

---

1. For more on definitions of corruption see Heidenheimer 1999.

a necessary instrument for winning elections.[2] In the making of their electoral strategies it is up to politicians to evaluate the exact value of corruption and anticorruption as political resources. In democratic politics corruption is a mechanism to raise campaign money and to control loyalties that can be critical for electoral success (Della Porta and Vannucci, 1999: 22–23).

The loans-for-shares scheme that was implemented in Russia in 1995 is the most powerful illustration of the functioning of corruption as an electoral resource. In the fall of 1995 public opinion polls indicated that the reelection of President Yeltsin was a mission impossible. His approval ratings were desperately low; the rejection of his politics and personality were overwhelming. In order to get reelected Yeltsin was searching for a powerful political constituency to support his bid. This is where loans-for-shares schemes came in. In the words of Chrystia Freeland "the loans-for-shares deal was a crude trade of property for political support. In exchange for some of Russia's most valuable companies, a group of businessmen—the oligarchs—threw their political muscle behind the Kremlin. ... The complicated two-step plan implicitly bound the economic fortunes of the future oligarchs

---

2. Della Porta and Vannucci (1999) have demonstrated that the rise of the "business politicians" who abuse power for personal enrichment was the result of a decision by the political parties to make selling public decisions the core of party activity.

to the political fortunes of the Yeltsin administration. In the autumn of 1995, the businessmen received stakes in Russia's most valuable companies only in trust. The final, formal transfer of ownership would not take place until the autumn of 1996 and in 1997 —after the presidential elections. When he signed the decree, the Kremlin chief bought himself the constituency which a year later would guarantee his reelection" (Freeland, 2000: 162, 173).

But corruption can have a high political cost. A growing number of governments lost reelection as a result of devastating corruption scandals (Blankenburg, 2002). Generally, voters do not like corrupt politicians. It is voters' perception of corruption as a social evil that makes not only corruption but also anticorruption a political resource. In a country where the public does not perceive corruption as morally wrong anticorruption is not such a resource. This is the weakness of the anticorruption campaigns in some African countries (De Sardan, 1999). At the same time, the stronger the moral rejection of corruption the higher the risks of corruption-centered politics and the stronger the incentives for anticorruption politics. Polling data in Bulgaria in the last decade indicate that the increase in public concern with corruption leads to an increase in support for the opposition parties regardless of which party is in power and which is in opposition.

In asking whether non-corrupt governments have incentives to launch anticorruption campaigns, we define a non-corrupt government as a government that is not seeking reelection through corruption-centered politics. A non-corrupt government in this sense means neither incorruptible government (nobody dares to think about it), nor clean government or honest government. It refers to a government that is convinced that it cannot be reelected through a corruption-related strategy and has consciously decided not to rely on such a strategy. The government estimates that raising party funds and buying political support through corruption will be politically more costly than not raising this money. In the classical case a non-corrupt government is a government that comes to power after several governments relying on corruption schemes failed to be reelected.

Launching an anticorruption campaign reflects the decision of a government to mobilize anticorruption sentiments as an electoral resource. An anticorruption campaign is not simply a mix of anticorruption policies. An anticorruption campaign is a governmental strategy that defines corruption as the major problem faced by the country and formulates the reduction of corruption as the major policy objective of the government. In our specific case the campaign includes the implementation of a World Bank designed set of anticorruption policies and the use of anticorruption rhetoric to justify policy decisions of the government. In this sense the implementation of the anticorruption policy package in the absence of anticorruption rhetoric does not qualify as a campaign.

The question this paper explores is whether non-corrupt governments have incentives to launch anticorruption campaigns as means for reelection. In other words, do non-corrupt governments have an interest to define corruption as the major problem of their country and to use anticorruption rhetoric as a pillar of their reelection strategy?

The argument is developed as a case study of one country—Bulgaria. The limited validity of the findings prevents us from coming to any general conclusion. But we believe that isolated cases can help produce radical rethinking of the existing policy paradigms.

The Case

The June 17, 2001 parliamentary elections were a breaking point for the Bulgarian political system. The results were surprising, shocking, and exotic. National Movement Simeon II, a political party that had been founded by Bulgarian ex-king Simeon Saxe-Coburg-Gotha just three months prior to the elections won a majority in the Bulgarian Parliament (Bárány, 2002). It won a majority in every age, education, and income group and in every region of the country with the exception of the regions with a compact Turkish population. The internationally praised Union of Democratic Forces (UDF) government of Ivan Kostov was bitterly defeated. According to many observers, the UDF government's corruption was the most convincing explanation for the electoral revolution/restoration of the former king (Bárány, 2002).

Corruption cleanups and promises of a politics of morality were central elements of the king's election victory. The new government formed in July 2001 was composed of political newcomers. None of the ministers had former governmental experience. None was connected with the political machines of the traditional parties. None had any record of corruption.

The situation that emerged on the day after the Bulgarian elections came close to a perfect opportunity for the implementation of a successful anticorruption campaign. It fits what the World Bank defines as "window of opportunity" (World Bank 2000, pp. xxviii, 69). Almost all components needed for a successful anticorruption campaign were present. There was a corrupt country. There was an election promise to clean up the system. There was a new reformist government that was a crusading outsider to corrupt politics. The new government was not a hostage of its own party machine because there was practically no party behind it. There was a carefully designed anticorruption policy package prepared by the international donors waiting to be implemented. There was an active anticorruption NGO community consolidated in an umbrella organization called Coalition 2000.

Bulgaria was a dream case not only for starting an anticorruption campaign; it was also a dream opportunity for empirically testing the chances for success of such a campaign. Since 1998 the Center for the Study of Democracy and Vitosha Research, an independent polling agency, had conducted 15 different polls tracing the anticorruption attitudes in the country. The method used was face-to-face interviews. Twelve of the surveys were based on the same questionnaire that allowed the construction of a detailed picture of the dynamics and specifics of the corruption reality in Bulgaria and the support for anticorruption politics. Three of the surveys studied a sizable sample of specific social groups—politicians, public officials, and businessmen.[3] The surveys culminated in the construction of several indeces through which to monitor the corruption reality in the country. The closer the value of indeces is to 10, the more negative are the assessments of the evaluated aspects of corruption in Bulgaria. Index numbers closer to 0 indicate the approximation to the ideal of a "corruption free" society. The indeces that are most interesting for us are:

- Index of corruption pressure: it measures the spread of attempts of employees in the public sector to directly or indirectly try to put pressure on citizens to give monetary gifts or services;
- Index of corruption practices: it reflects the level of personal participation of respondents in different forms of corrupt behavior (e.g. paying a bribe);
- Index of the perceived spread of corruption: it registers citizens' subjective assessments of the spread of corruption through society;

---

3. See Vitosha Research's website:
www.vitosha-research.com.

• Index of corruption expectations: it represents citizens' personal expectations about the future spread of corruption and its perspectives.[4]

The first two of the indices can be viewed as trying to measure corruption reality, to capture how many times bribes were demanded and/or offered. The last two can be viewed as representing the public perceptions about the phenomenon. It needs to be recognized here that the measurement of both corruption reality and corruption perceptions is problematic, and the four indices may systematically deviate from the true values they are trying to measure. More specifically, it is natural for measurements of corruption reality to have a downward bias due to a tendency for respondents to public surveys to underreport corrupt acts they have experienced, and for measurements of corruption perceptions to have an upward bias due to a habit to use corruption as an explanation for various events and processes. At the same time, if these biases are relatively stable through time, the changes in the indices should reflect reality without much bias. As figure 1 shows, in the case of Bulgaria the two sets of variables differ significantly not only in their levels (which is to be expected as a result of the biases in their measurement), but also in their dynamics over a period of almost five years.

----

4. For fuller details see
   www.anticorruption.bg/index_eng.php.

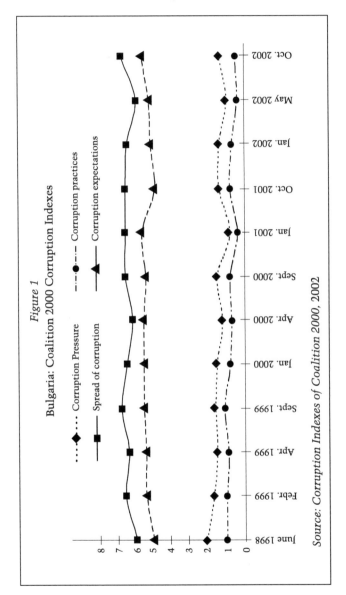

Figure 1

Bulgaria: Coalition 2000 Corruption Indexes

Corruption Pressure
Corruption practices
Corruption expectations
Spread of corruption

Source: Corruption Indexes of Coalition 2000, 2002

Between April and June 2002 the Open Society Foundation in Bulgaria in collaboration with the Centre for Liberal Strategies and Alfa Research conducted a "State of Society" survey combining representative public opinion survey with anthropological fieldwork in the country.[5] The research goal was to reveal citizens' interpretations of the meaning of transition: who won, who lost and what happened to winners and losers. The survey was especially interested in anticorruption attitudes and anticorruption discourses, as a mechanism used by the respondents to rationalize their transition experience.

These two massive blocks of data form the empirical basis of this study. We try to answer the question —Did the newly elected Bulgarian government have incentives to seek reelection through anticorruption campaigns?—by interpreting the findings of these two surveys.

The limitations of the suggested approach are significant. In order to use the data as an opportunity to study the incentives of the government to launch an anticorruption campaign we presume that the dynamics between reported corruption experience and corruption perceptions will remain the same after starting an energetic anticorruption campaign. Our focus on the government and not the individual politicians as vote maximizers also invites uneasy questions. The fact that Bulgaria has a party government elected

---

5. See report at www.osf.bg/sos.

through the system of proportional representation makes such an assumption legitimate, but it still can raise a lot of problems. Theoretically we cannot exclude the possibility of a non-corrupt government composed of corrupt politicians who do not use corruption as an electoral resource but use it simply as means for personal enrichment.

The major justification for our approach is the intuition that in order to convince a prime minister to start an anticorruption campaign, you should convince his election strategist. And the strategist will not miss the chance to read the existing empirical data on the subject.

We first draw up a fictional conversation in the office of the prime minister where an advocate of initiating an anticorruption campaign (e.g. a World Bank expert) and an opponent of such a campaign (e.g. an election strategist) are exchanging views. We then reflect on the dynamics of the anticorruption sentiments through the perspective of social constructivism and draw some conclusions.

The Prime Minister's Dilemma

It is one of those rainy days when governments wished they were honest. The date of the meeting is obscure because most questions asked are the same as the ones that were the most relevant in late summer 2001, but some of the empirical data presented cover later periods. So, we do not specify when the meeting takes place.

Let us imagine that the prime minister (formerly a king) has gathered the members of his cabinet, and the purpose of the meeting is to decide whether the new Bulgarian government should build its reelection strategy on an anticorruption campaign. Let us also imagine the following: there are two points of view—the proponents' and the opponents' of an anticorruption campaign; the speakers are closet social scientists; the prime minister is not only an ex-king but also an ex-dean of a social sciences department; the prime minister is sick of normative arguments and insists that their decision should be based on the available empirical data.

There are many more things to imagine in constructing a fictional conversation in the Bulgarian Oval Office. But there is a basic limitation: the government can only rely on the resources controlled by the executive power and its parliamentary majority. The government cannot rely on an efficient and impartial judicial power as an ally in the war against corruption. The European Union (EU) Report on the state of judicial reform in Bulgaria confirms such an assumption realistic (European Commission, 2002). The pressure of the international community will also be disclosed from the discussion. A situation when the incentives created by the EU accession process can have a critical weight in the government's decision to start an anticorruption campaign and that the signals coming from the EU can have a decisive impact on voters' behavior can also be imagined. But for making our major argument stronger, we omit these factors.

Another important assumption is that the World Bank's anticorruption policy package works. Let us imagine that implementing these policies will lead to a reduction in the actual levels of corruption and will have positive effects on the economy. Of course, some of the anticorruption policies suggested by the World Bank may be wrong and misconceived. There is a growing literature criticizing different elements of the anticorruption policy package (Stiglitz, 2002; Easterly, 2001). But this paper is not about policies. It is about incentives. That is why we imagine a working anticorruption package that results in an actual decrease in the levels of corruption.

One might say that all these assumptions and limitations make the paper an unreliable guide to the real functioning of Bulgarian politics after June 2001. But our purpose is not to be Vergilius in the inferno of Bulgarian politics. What we are interested in are the policy implications of the elusive nature of corruption.

Let us now summarize the discussion in the prime minister's Oval Office. It is sanitized of emotions and details. The goal is to present the main arguments in a concise and clear form. The arguments of the opponent of an anticorruption campaign are presented at greater length because they are new to the ministers and because they are closer to the views of the authors.

Why Should Governments Launch Anticorruption Campaigns?

The Economic Argument. Recent literature on corruption[6] has reached several conclusions about the effects of corruption on the economy and on the economic state of society, using both theoretical arguments and empirical studies of various samples of countries. The advocate of launching an anticorruption campaign, who treats them as almost established facts, makes extensive use of some of these conclusions.

First, corruption hurts economic growth. It does so by hurting investments and by distorting the allocation of resources towards inefficiency. Corruption means that the rules of economic activity are arbitrarily imposed, that property rights are insecure, and that the administrative capacity to provide services is low, which translates into a highly uncertain business environment (World Bank, 1997: 18–20). Uncertainty raises the costs of private investment and hurts the growth of productive capacity. At the same time, corruption impedes the effectiveness of public investment (Tanzi and Davoodi, 1997)—it leads to higher public investment outlays combined with lower productivity of these investments. Corruption also hurts prospects for foreign direct investment, especially in

---

6. A concise summary can be found at World Bank 2000: 18–24.

Bulgaria, which is poor in natural resources that could attract investors despite corruption (World Bank, 2000: 23, note 2). On the other side, corruption decreases the efficiency of resource allocation by introducing severe distortions into the price system (Shleifer and Vishny, 1993: 599–617) and also, by creating incentives for lower budget revenues and higher budget expenditures, creating an unsustainable fiscal position (Tanzi and Davoodi, 1997; World Bank, 2000: 21–22) which results in high inflation and again in lower effectiveness of the price system. The impact on the price system results in a misallocation of resources towards suboptimal uses. Ultimately, low investments and poor allocation of resources spell low growth in the long run.

Second, corruption not only hurts the long-term welfare of people, but it does so in an unfair way. The costs associated with corruption fall mostly on the weakest and most vulnerable groups in society. Corrupt societies experience more poverty and higher inequality than non-corrupt ones. This is due not only to lower growth, but to the fact that corrupt governments get effectively financed through regressive, rather than progressive taxes, that they cannot effectively establish and maintain social safety nets, and that they divert resources away from investment in human and social capital, both of which are important for reducing poverty and inequality (Gupta, Davoodi, and Alonso-Terme, 1998; World Bank 2000: 20–21).

Third, corruption is a factor for the erosion of trust in institutions, and thereof in the social fabric in general. Corruption leads to lower budget revenues and to higher but much less productive budget expenditures, which justifies people thinking that they are paying more for less. Moreover, it is mostly the poor and the disadvantaged who pay the bill, but get almost nothing from the services that they are in fact financing. Logically, this leads to a very low level of public trust in state organs and in political leaders, thus further reducing the capacity of the state to provide welfare enhancing services (Shleifer and Vishny, 1993; Gupta et al., 1998; Tanzi and Davoodi, 1997; Tanzi, 1998; World Bank, 2000: 21–22).

The conclusion that can be drawn from the literature on anticorruption is that a successful anticorruption strategy will result in a better performing economy which means higher growth, higher and more fairly distributed incomes and will raise the capacity of the state to provide efficient public services and further improve the well-being of society.

Ultimately, the logic of the economic argument is that the government's incentives to launch an anticorruption campaign are rooted in the understanding of the damaging economic effects of corruption. If corruption is defeated, these damages will disappear, people will feel their lives improve and will vote accordingly.

The Political Argument. The economic argument demonstrates the advantages that any government can have from reducing corruption. But it does not address the problem of why the government should employ anticorruption rhetoric and why it should focus its efforts on convincing the public that corruption has been reduced. The vacuum left by the economic argument is filled by the political argument. What has so far been discussed is not the damage that corruption does to democracy (Rose-Ackerman, 1999; della Porta and Vannucci, 1999). The argument has focused on the importance of corruption as an electoral issue. The results of recent surveys demonstrate that in the public view corruption is one of the three basic problems the country faces. So, it is unrealistic to play down corruption as a political issue. It is not only corruption but the public's perception of the country's being corrupt that can hurt the reelection chances of the government.

The very nature of post-ideological politics increases the importance of corruption as an electoral issue. The decline of ideology led to the rise in the importance of the personal integrity of those in power. The EU accession process significantly limits the policy choices any "reasonable" government should follow in the period of transition, thus increasing the importance of the moral image of the government still further.

In a sense some influential elite groups (such as journalists and civil society activists) portray corruption in terms of what Cohen called "moral panic" (1972). A "moral panic" is said to exist when a particular condition comes to be defined as a threat to societal values and interests and when its nature, consequences, and solutions are presented by influential elites in "a stylized and stereotypical fashion" (Pavarala, 1996: 134).

There are two additional practical arguments in favor of an anticorruption campaign that are specific to the present Bulgarian government. An anticorruption campaign can strengthen its image as the government of political novices who were not involved in the great redistribution of the last decade. Being in power for the first time, the government is perfectly positioned to attack and expose the corruption of previous governments thus undermining the electoral chances of the opposition insofar as it represents the parties of the previous governments.

More importantly, there were public expectations that the government would undertake decisive steps against corruption. In September 2001 the corruption expectation index changed in a positive direction regardless of the fact that both corruption practices and corruption pressures went in the opposite direction. This change can be explained only as a direct result of the June election. The index on the moral acceptability of corruption also demonstrates that public opinion is not inclined to trivialize the existence of corruption (see figure 2 which shows the index of moral acceptability of corruption with 0 meaning corruption is declared absolutely unacceptable, and 10 meaning it is declared as acceptable).

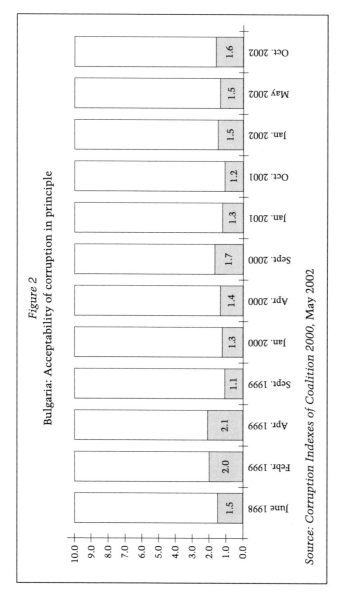

Figure 2
Bulgaria: Acceptability of corruption in principle

Source: Corruption Indexes of Coalition 2000, May 2002

On the contrary, corruption is perceived as a moral evil. There is a strong majority that is not ready to tolerate corruption. Anticorruption politics could be a major electoral resource.

Why should the Government Not Launch an Anti-corruption Campaign? The presentation by the opponent of an anticorruption campaign was a surprise to most of the ministers. He did not question any of the arguments of the proponent of the anticorruption politics. He made only one point: the realm of corruption and the realm of anticorruption sentiments are two parallel worlds and governments cannot change short-term perceptions of corruption even if their anticorruption policies are succeeding in reducing actual corruption.

In his view, in electoral terms a success in the war against corruption means that people are convinced that corruption has significantly decreased and that the prospects of eliminating corruption have increased. In other words, the success of an anticorruption campaign in the language of our study means that the anticorruption campaign should produce visible changes in the corruption perceived spread index and the corruption expectations index.

The major argument of the opponent of anticorruption campaigns and the major argument of this paper is that even the successful implementation of anticorruption policies is unlikely to produce such a change. The evidence is that the actual decline in the level of corruption measured by corruption pressure

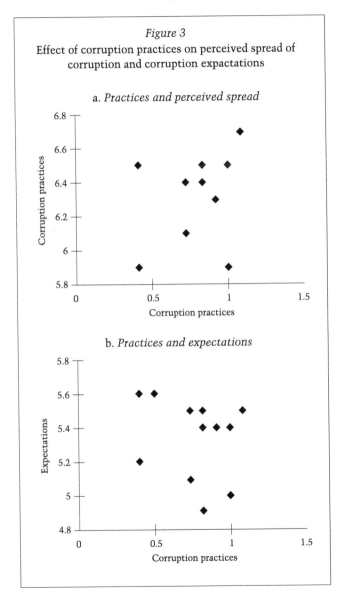

Figure 3
Effect of corruption practices on perceived spread of
corruption and corruption expactations

a. *Practices and perceived spread*

b. *Practices and expectations*

and corruption practices indeces fail to correlate with a significant decline in the corruption perceived spread and corruption expectation indeces. If votes are based on perceptions of corruption rather than on personal experience, this presents a problem for democratic reformers.

The assumption of those advocating anticorruption campaigns is that the public will "feel" the actual reduction of corruption, and the government will be politically rewarded. This assumption has never been tested. The reading of the existing Bulgarian data on the corruption attitudes of people does not support this assumption.

Figure 3 shows scatter plots of the observation points of corruption practices and corruption perceived spread indices (on the left axis) and the observation points of corruption practices and corruption expectations indices (on the right axis) for the 12 surveys performed by Vitosha Research. The graphic evidence suggests that the corruption practice index does not correlate either with the corruption perceived spread index or the corruption expectation index.

The data also indicate that the corruption pressure index does not correlate with the corruption perceived spread index or corruption expectation index (see the scatter plots linking the corruption pressure index with the two perception indices in figure 4).

The statistical link between the two sets of variables is very weak, which is exactly the opposite of what the advocates of anticorruption campaigns imagine. The dynamics of the corruption reality variables

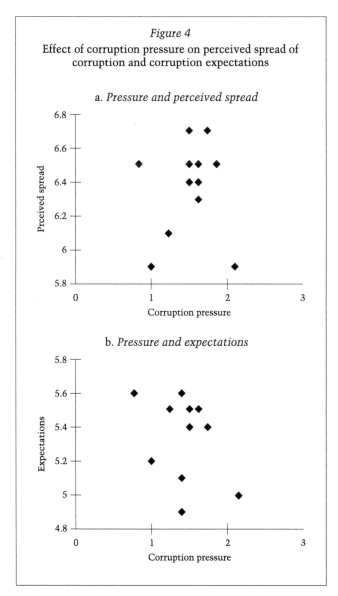

Figure 4
Effect of corruption pressure on perceived spread of
corruption and corruption expectations

a. *Pressure and perceived spread*

b. *Pressure and expectations*

have no explanatory power for the dynamics of the corruption perception variables even with a lag of one observation.

In other words the opinion of the people on the spread of corruption in the country and their expectations on the further spread of the phenomenon are not formed on the base of their personal experience. Neither bribes they were asked to pay, nor bribes that they gave or were given to them shaped their opinion on the spread of corruption.

Different interpretations of this unexpected result are possible but the most obvious one is that when citizens judge the spread of corruption in the country, this is not a judgment on the level of administrative corruption that they encounter in everyday life, but it is a judgment on the political corruption.

The basic problem that arises from our initial findings is that the public has difficulty "learning" that corruption has decreased and perceptions are weakly correlated with experiences. This finding is also confirmed by looking at a cross-section of individual respondents' data. When the full panel of observations is taken into account, the correlations between the two corruption reality and the two corruption perception variables are between 0.1 and 0.22.[7]

In this sense the legitimate question is whether the public can learn about the reduced level of corruption through the media if it cannot learn through

---

7. We are grateful to Vitosha Research for this information.

personal experience. This is an essential question in deciding whether to go or not to go for an anticorruption campaign. It is obvious that in an environment of low trust in institutions, the public will not "trust" government when it claims success in reducing corruption. It is also obvious that if the government makes the reduction of corruption its priority, the opposition will have more incentives to attack the government for being corrupt and to claim that corruption has increased (this is what actually is happening in Bulgaria these days). Can the media be the channel through which the truth about the levels of corruption will reach the public?

The empirical data suggest that there is a strong correlation between the number of corruption related publications in a certain period and increases in the corruption perceived spread index. That means that the more media writes about corruption the more people tend to believe that the level of corruption in their country has increased. The logical question is how the content of published articles influences this finding. The fact that there is a competitive media market in Bulgaria that does not have a visible ideological bias, and the fact that this market is dominated by foreign-owned media could be a precondition that informed citizens will get the truth even if the opposition or other enemies of the government will make false accusations trying to discredit government policies. But is media competition a safeguard for truth?

Empirically it is simply impossible to test how

many of the major corruption scandals that hit the front pages revealed real cases of corruption and in what proportion they represent the clever use of corruption accusations for political or business purposes. The nonfunctioning judicial system makes such a test a nonoption.

But the question of whether media competition neutralizes media bias is not confined to the coverage of corruption. So we adopt the argument constructed in Shleifer's and Mullainathan's recent article "Media Bias" (2002). They distinguish two different types of media bias. One of them, which they refer to as ideology, reflects a news outlet's desire to affect readers' opinion in a particular direction. The other one, which they refer to as spin, reflects the outlet's attempt simply to create a memorable story, thus selling more copies. The authors examined a theoretical model of competition among media outlets in the presence of these biases. What they demonstrated is that whereas under the model competition eliminates the effect of the ideological bias, it actually exaggerates the incentives to spin stories. In other words, if the media market is dominated by spin bias, as is the case in Bulgaria, Shleifer and Mullainathan's results would suggest that competition will increase the incentives of news outlets to report stories in a way that meets the expectations of their readers which will strengthen the assumptions of the first reporting.

The conclusion of this analysis is that a governmental anticorruption campaign will increase and not decrease the number of corruption-related stories and that media competition instead of correcting the anti-governmental bias and the fake nature of some corruption accusations will tend to exaggerate this trend. In other words the position of the media will be that any story that possibly could be a corruption story will be told as a proven corruption story. And that any story that was initially covered as a corruption story will tend to continue to be covered as a corruption story. More explicitly, media competition will side with corruption accusations even when the facts proving these accusations are of a doubtful nature.

The case of the "the corrupt executive director of Bulgartabak" is a powerful illustration of the effects of spin bias. In the fall of 2001 the new Bulgarian government decided to appoint a new executive director to Bulgartabak, the Bulgarian tobacco company. Bulgartabak is a big state-owned enterprise, which was scheduled for privatization in 2002. The government's decision to make this appointment was based on its desire to limit the temptation for inside dealings in the critical year when the enterprise was going to be privatized. It was a logical decision. The enterprise was known as a source of illegal party financing of more than one party. The government's choice for executive director was a young Bulgarian whose entire career had been with multinational companies outside of Bulgaria. His previous work had nothing to do with the tobacco industry. The appointment provoked sensational interest when information was leaked to the press that the new director had negotiated a western type salary, many times higher than the salary of the previous director.[8] For a month the government denied that such a salary was negotiated.

A month later representatives of one of the partners of Bulgartabak and candidate buyers of the enterprise wrote a letter to the prime minister accusing the executive director of asking for a 500,000 dollar bribe in a confidential meeting in a notorious restaurant. The accusers reported that they had had the conversation taped and were ready to give the tapes to the prosecutor. For several weeks the media covered the case extensively, openly favoring the accusing side. As a result of the media pressure, the director was replaced. This story could be an example of the important role of the media in revealing corruption cases. But it could also serve as an example of how spin bias works to the disadvantage of the government.

The story has its other side. The accusing party turned out to be very close to a well-known Russian businessman who was expelled from Bulgaria as a threat to national security; he never gave evidence for their accusations. The famous tapes which recorded the corrupt offer were never presented to the prosecutor.

Is, then, the Bulgartabak director a classical case of a corrupt official or is he a classical victim of a kompromat campaign whose aim was to oust the unfriendly director? The question looks difficult to

---

8. The Centre for Liberal Strategies has a project tracking specific corruption-related cases, including media coverage. See www.cls-sofia.org.

resolve, but the public unanimously made up its mind. The investigation was closed for lack of evidence, but public opinion pronounced its sentence: the director's resignation was a confession from the government that their man was corrupt. For the government, the removal of the suspected director was the only way to prove that it had been serious in its decision to fight corruption. In the words of Ákos Szilágyi "you cannot argue with kompromat, nor can you refute it. There is only one adequate response to kompromat, i.e., counter-kompromat" (2002: 219).

Making our argument stronger, we claim that the government's focus on corruption increases the incentives of the opposition to attack the government for being corrupt. Shleifer's argument demonstrates why in the Bulgarian media environment the government has little chance to defend itself. The fact that it takes years for any libel suit to be settled only strengthens this conclusion. The anticorruption campaign can easily turn into a kompromat war.

In short, the government does not have real instruments to change the indeces of the perceived spread of corruption and of corruption expectations, which, we assume, are precisely the indices that have to change if the government is to be reelected. This is the major finding of our reading of the empirical data. As we have pointed out above, the world of corruption perceptions and the world of corruption are two parallel worlds. What matters are the policy implications of this unexpected finding.

What Is the Problem with Anticorruption Campaigns?
The Social Constructionist Perspective. Governments'
disincentives to undertake anticorruption campaigns
are related to the elusive nature of the corruption as a
policy issue. This finding suggests the need for additional reflection on the nature of corruption and corruption perceptions in transition.

Recently, the debate on the "special nature" of
corruption as a social problem took the form of a debate on the measurability of corruption (Sik, 2002;
Krastev, 2002). The construction of the Transparency
International (TI) corruption perception index gave
rise to a new generation of studies on the effects of
corruption (Lambsdorff, 1999). In these studies TI perception indeces were treated as hard data. But what
do we measure when we measure corruption? Do we
measure the number of bribes per person in a country?
Do we measure the number of people being involved
in corrupt transactions? Do we measure the volume
of money that circulates in corrupt exchanges? Do
we measure which levels of political power are captured by special interests? But in the final analysis,
the major problem with measuring corruption is its
secret nature—all parties involved in a corrupt transaction have an incentive to hide it.

The measurement debate turned anticorruption
studies away from another important aspect of corruption's elusiveness and away from the problem of
how corruption has been constructed as a policy problem in different societies. Whose definition of the
causes, culprits and solutions of the corruption prob-

lem has been accepted? Who wins and who loses in the definitions war? It should not be surprising that "groups with conflicting interests and stakes in the system have varied perspectives on the nature of the problem and compete with one another to impose their particular constructions and influence the public discourse on the subject" (Pavarala, 1996: 19).

Governments and international donors have defined corruption primarily as an institutional problem and have assumed that the public accepts the same definition of the causes and cures for the corruption phenomenon. But the consensus on the causes, effects, and solution of corruption turned out to be an illusionary one. In judging the success of anticorruption campaigns, the average citizen adopts his own perspective on the causes of corruption, its effects, and what constitutes successful anticorruption politics. And his perspective is not an institutional one. The definitions endorsed by the public are more broadly moralistic than narrowly legalistic, and they tend to be more individual centered than institutional. The public is more interested in fixing the responsibility than in analyzing the phenomenon.

In this respect only the social constructionist point of view can explain the fact that the corruption perception index does not reflect changes in the reported level of corruption. The critical problem is how to interpret the misrepresentation of the corruption phenomenon in Bulgaria. The nature of this misrepresentation is more important for designing anticorruption strategies than the actual levels of corruption.

The empirical data collected by Vitosha Research covered not only the corruption perceptions of the population as a whole, but in three occasions the agency has also studied the corruption perceptions of sizable samples of public officials, politicians, and businessmen. What is interesting for us is to understand how these four groups—the public, the politician, the public official, and the businessman—define the causes of corruption. What is the dynamic of their explanations, and whose definitions are winning the day?

In this respect we can distinguish between three basic constructions of the causes of corruption: (1) corruption is an institutional issue, and it can be reduced by institutional changes—withdrawing the state from the economy, more transparency and accountability, introduction of new legislation; (2) corruption is an economic phenomenon, it is the result of inadequate payments in the public sector; (3) corruption is a political problem—it is an instrument for politicians to enrich themselves at the expense of the majority of the population, and it is rooted in the selection of the political elite. Almost no one views corruption as a cultural problem. It is not surprising that the public, politicians, bureaucrats, and businessmen each predominantly favor one of these constructions. Politicians promote the institutional view of the causes of corruption and push for institutional solutions. Public officials endorse economic explanation for the spread of corruption, referring to the low salaries of public officials and the political pressures on the bureaucracy. Their preferable solution is higher salaries and higher punishment. At the beginning of the monitored period they tended to support the economic explanation of the causes of corruption. With the acceleration of the privatization process in 1999, they turned to a different explanation—it arose from the nature and the project of the political elite. For the general public, the question what causes corruption was replaced by the question who benefits from corruption. The public's preferable solution is a change in the political elite, so that all other anticorruption policies are peripheral. This coincides with the public's criticism of the existing electoral system based on proportional representation and the constantly declining trust in the political parties. The businessmen have no view in common. They recognize the institutional nature of the problem but are ready to blame politicians for the state of corruption. What is interesting is that all four groups view themselves as the primary victims of corruption.

In our view the fact that the political elite lost the definition war and failed to convert the public to see the institutional nature of the corruption phenomenon is at the heart of the cognitive split between the personal experience of corruption and the shaping of corruption perceptions. The government and the public are operating with two different definitions of the causes of corruption and its cures. To the extent that public opinion defines corruption as the very nature of exercising power, attempts of the government to convince the public of its efforts to clean up the system will fail to confront the accusations of the opposition that this government is even more corrupt than the previous one.

There are two cases that illustrate the policy implications of the public's definition of corruption. The Privatization Agency is traditionally ranked among the most corrupt institutions in Bulgaria. What is unexpected is that businessmen who are more familiar with the work of the agency tend to view it less corrupt than the general public which is at an arm's length away from it. Where does this discrepancy come from? If our interpretation of the meaning of the post-communist perceptions of corruption is correct, then business people judge the corruption of the privatization process, while the general public sees the Privatization Agency as the agent of corruption because privatization itself is perceived as one of the sublime manifestations of post-communist corruption. For the public, the Privatization Agency is corrupt not because its representatives take bribes and rig procedures, but because as an elite project, privatization is by definition identical with corruption. It is an instrument for the elite to steal from the public through the state.

The case of the customs office is even more striking. If the institutional view of the political usefulness of anticorruption campaigns is taken seriously, it has to rely on a link between institutional performance and corruption perceptions. The Bulgarian Customs Agency provides a very indicative example. From the very beginning of the corruption surveys in 1997 respondents perceived the customs office as the most

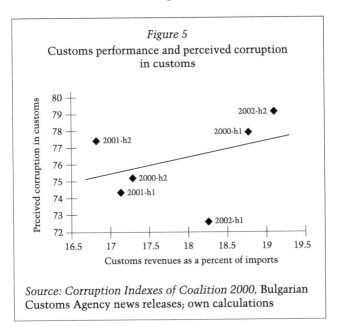

Figure 5
Customs performance and perceived corruption
in customs

Source: *Corruption Indexes of Coalition 2000,* Bulgarian
Customs Agency news releases; own calculations

corrupt institution in the country. Assuming that improved institutional performance will be rewarded by lower corruption perceptions and that institutional performance depends on institutional incentives, in the fall of 2001 the king's government opted for the radical solution of putting the agency under the supervision of a foreign private company (the British company Crown Agents). The media massively covered the governmental initiative.

It is too early to tell whether the new arrangement will lead to an improved institutional performance by the Bulgarian customs. However, corruption surveys conducted both before and after Crown Agents took over in early 2002 indicate that public perceptions about the level of corruption in the customs is positively, rather than negatively, correlated with the performance of the agency measured by total customs revenues (customs collect not only tariffs, but value added and excise taxes at the point of entry as well) as a percent of total imports. This is illustrated in figure 5 using six-month periodicity for 2000–2002.

The fact that the periods of most successful institutional performance (in the first half of 2000 and in the second half of 2002) correspond to the highest level of public perception about corruption in the customs is especially telling. Obviously, the Bulgarian public did not define corruption primarily as an institutional problem.

Reading the data leads to the conclusion that it is highly unlikely that the public infers the level of corruption based on institutional performance. Again, it is much more likely that for the public the problem with corruption is the problem with the elite, with the shared belief that "politicians are crooks" and with the criminalization of politics as public activity. The results of the "State of Society" survey in a different way confirmed these findings. The survey portrayed Bulgaria as a classical "us versus them" society where the vast majority of people experienced the time of transition as a time of economic and status loss.

In trying to rationalize the loss of income and social status, different social groups formulate different claims on the definition, consequences, and preconditions for corruption. The losers of the reforms tend to define corruption as the very essence of the exercise of power. This explains some important differences in citizens' perception of the causes of corruption. The majority of losers view the causes of corruption in the nature and the projects of the power elites. In the view of the losers the transition is a zero sum game where they are the victims of a huge conspiracy. For them, transition is the period when elites have abandoned their social responsibilities. This definition of the nature of the transition explains why the majority of citizens defined politicians and criminals as the real winners of the change and why they defined people like themselves as the real losers.

The described situation is not specific only to Bulgaria. In their comparative study of the social psychological objectives on the way to a market economy in Eastern and Central Europe a group of Hungarian sociologists have demonstrated that "The public, after the collapse of state socialism in 1989–90, was shocked by the abruptness and depth of the transition and took shelter behind moral ideas thought to be safe. But from that vantage point, the economic transition seemed even more repugnant. Looking at the transition in terms of justice, trustworthiness, and confidence, people discerned corruption, untrustworthiness, injustice, and undeserved enrichment by a new elite, whereas in most cases, nothing had really happened beyond the normal functioning of the market" (Csepeli et al., 2004).

The public, after the collapse of state socialism in 1989–90, was shocked by the abruptness and depth of the transition and took shelter behind moral ideas thought to be safe. But from that vantage point, the economic transition seemed even more repugnant. Looking at the transition in terms of justice, trustworthiness and confidence, people discerned corruption, untrustworthiness, injustice, and undeserved enrichment by a new elite, whereas in most cases, nothing had really happened beyond the normal functioning of the market.

Losing the war on the meaning of the transition, the political elites have come under siege. In the opinion of the public the economic transition is perceived as a zero-sum game where the enrichment and success of some people could be attained only at the expense and loss of others. This explanatory interpretative scheme came just at the right moment for those who perceived themselves as losers, because they could explain their own failure by undeserved enrichment of the others.

In this sense the index of the perceived spread of corruption reflects much more the lost war on the meaning of transition and the lack of legitimacy of the new market rules than the actual level of bribery. And this makes it an inappropriate policy objective.

Conclusions

The interpretation of the dynamics of the politics of corruption perceptions in Bulgaria invites unexpected conclusions. The findings of this paper could be read simply as a Bulgarian pathology. It could be read as an example of the particular nature of corruption perceptions in the transition countries. But they could also be viewed as an example of a general problem with anticorruption politics.

Our most obvious policy conclusion is that non-contextual policy advice creates enormous risks for the political process in the host country. In the case of Bulgaria the idea of launching an anticorruption campaign looks unattractive to "the highest levels of government" because initiating such a campaign does not contribute to the reelection of the government. The assumption that non-corrupt governments have incentives to initiate anticorruption campaigns turned out to be a wrong one. Anticorruption campaigns contribute to the delegitimization of the elites and to the destabilization of the political system. Non-corrupt governments do not have incentives to start anticorruption campaigns because they do not have chances to convince the public that they are successful in fighting corruption. The popular perception of corruption reflects much more the dynamics of the public's dissatisfaction with the current state of affairs than the actual levels of bribery. The consequence is that institution-based anticorruption campaigns were swayed by other features of the transition. The findings of the paper suggest that it would be more productive to pursue anticorruption policies avoiding anticorruption rhetoric as a major instrument for justifying reform policies.

References

Bárány, Zoltán. 2002. "Bulgaria's Royal Election." Journal of Democracy 13:141–55.

Blankenburg, Erhard. 2002. "From Political Clientelism to Outright Corruption—The Rise of the Scandal Industry." In S. Kotkin and A. Sajó (eds.). Political Corruption in Transition. A Skeptic's Handbook, pp. 149–66. Budapest, New York: Central European University Press.

Cohen, Stanley. 1972. Folk Devils and Moral Panics: The Creation of the Mods and Rockers. London: MacGibbon and Kee/St.. Martin's Press.

Csepeli, György, Antal Örkény, Mária Székelyi, and Ildikó Barna. 2004. "Blindness to Success: Social Psychological Objectives along the Way to a Market Economy in Eastern Europe." In J. Kornai, B. Rothstein, and S. Rose-Ackerman (eds.). Creating Social Trust in Post-Socialist Transition, New York: Palgrave Macmillan, forthcoming.

Easterly, William. 2001. The Elusive Quest for Growth: Economists' Adventure and Misadventures in the Tropics. Cambridge, Mass: MIT Press.

European Commission. 2002. Regular Report on Bulgaria's Progress towards Accession. Brussels: The European Commission.

Freeland, Chrystia. 2000. Sale of the Century. The Inside Story of the Second Russian Revolution. London: Little, Brown and Company.

Gupta, Sanjeev, Hamid Davoodi, and Rosa Alonso-Terme. 1998. Does Corruption Affect Income Inequality and Poverty? IMF Working Paper No. 76. Washington D.C.: International Monetary Fund.

Haidenheimer, Arnold J. (ed.). 1999. Political Corruption: A Handbook, 5th ed. New Brunswick, N.J: Transaction Publication.

Krastev, Ivan. 2002. "A Moral Economy of Anticorruption Sentiments in Eastern Europe." In Y. Elkana, I. Krastev, E. Macamo, and S. Randeria (eds.). Unraveling Ties—From Social Cohesion to New Practices of Connectedness, pp. 99–117. Frankfurt, New York: Campus Verlag.

Lambsdorf, J. Graf. 1999. Corruption in Empirical Research—A Review. Paper presented at the 9th International Anti-corruption Conference (IACC) at Durban, South Africa, October 10–15. Available at www.transparency.org/iacc/9th_iacc/papers/day2/ws1/d2 ws1_jglambsdorff.html

Offe, Claus. 2002. Controlling Political Corruption: Conceptual and Practical Issues. Paper presented at Collegium Budapest conference, December 13–14. Available at http://www.colbud.hu/honesty-trust/offe/pub04.doc

Pavarala, Vihod. 1996. Interpreting Corruption. Elite Perspectives in India. New Delhi, Thousand Oaks, London: Sage Publications.

Della Porta, Donatella and Alberto Vannucci. 1999. Corrupt Exchanges. Actors, Resources, and Mechanisms of Political Corruption. New York: Aldine de Gruyter.

Rose-Ackerman, Susan. 1999. Corruption and Government: Causes, Consequences and Reform. Cambridge, UK: Cambridge University Press.

Sajó, András. 2002. "Clientelism and Extortion: Corruption in Transition." In S. Kotkin and A. Sajo (eds.). Political Corruption in Transition. A Skeptic's Handbook, pp. 1–22. Budapest, New York: Central European University Press.

de Sardan, Jean-Pierre Olivier. 1999. "A Moral Economy of Corruption in Africa." Journal of Modern African Studies 37:25–52.

Shleifer, Andrei and Robert Vishny. 1993. "Corruption." Quarterly Journal of Economics 108:599–618.

Shleifer, Andrei and Sendhil Mullainathan. 2002. Media Bias. NBER Working Paper No. 9295: National Bureau for Economic Research, Cambridge, MA
http://papers.nber.org/papers/w9295

Sik, Endre. 2002. "The Bad, the Worse and the Worst: Guesstimating the Level of Corruption." In S. Kotkin and A. Sajó (eds.). Political Corruption in Transition. A Skeptic's Handbook, pp. 91–114. Budapest, New York: Central European University Press.

Stiglitz, Joseph E. 2002. Globalization and Its Discontents. New York: W.W. Norton & Company.

Szilágyi, Ákos. 2002. "Kompromat and Corruption in Russia." In S. Kotkin and A. Sajo (eds.). Political Corruption in Transition. A Skeptic's Handbook, pp. 207–31. Budapest, New York: Central European University Press.

Tanzi, Vito. 1998. Corruption around the World: Causes, Consequences, Scope, and Cures. IMF Working Paper No. 63. Washington D.C.: International Monetary Fund.

Tanzi, Vito and Hamid Davoodi. 1997. Corruption, Public Investment, and Growth. IMF Working Paper No. 139. Washington D.C.: International Monetary Fund.

World Bank. 1997. Helping Counties Combat Corruption. The Role of The World Bank. Washington D.C.: World Bank.

World Bank. 2000. Anticorruption in Transition: A Contribution to the Policy Debate. Washington D.C.: World Bank.